Monsters' Throwdown

Monsters' Throwdown: A Human Odyssey

Eleanor L. Tomczyk

Published by Howthehelldidienduphere? Publications

ISBN: 1493616099
ISBN-13: 9781493616091
Library of Congress Control Number: 2013920570
CreateSpace Independent Publishing Platform
North Charleston, South Carolina

Dedication

Dedicated to "Pee-wee," CDT, KLT, and JRT: *To Pee-wee because you knew if we held on to each other, we'd be all right, and we'd make it through the fire swamp. To CDT and KLT because you taught me humility, and I greatly needed that as a mother and as a human being. Finally, this tale is dedicated to JRT because you promised to love me for better or for worse, and to restore all that the cankerworm had eaten. You kept those promises and then some, my handsome white knight.*

IN HONOR OF

Maggie M: *whose grace and courage led me out of ignorance, and whose embrace enveloped me in the arms of a loving mother where monsters cease to exist.*

Author's Note

~

This is a collection of absurdities in my life that form the arc of a memoir. Many of the conversations have been creatively reconstructed for the sake of a punch line. (No one remembers exactly what was said when they're four years old and dealing with crazy people, so it might as well be funny.) All the characters from my past have been hidden behind fictitious names and misidentifying characteristics because I don't want them coming back from the grave and haunting my ass. But overall, others who took this journey with me, and who have better memories than I have, vetted the manuscript and confirmed the veracity of my telling of the events that shaped my journey home to love.

Prologue

~

"My name is Nobody."— **The Odyssey,** by Homer

Sometimes being underestimated is a great way to get away from the monsters that are hell-bent on destroying you.

1

Hell, Thy Name Is Cleveland

~

"Life is pain, Highness! Anyone who says differently is selling something."—**The Princess Bride,** by William Goldman

Do you know what I've discovered about being born? It is not for the faint of heart. Even if you're born in the best of families with all your emotional and material needs set in place, it is pretty obvious from the beginning of every human's life that you're entering into a world of hurt.

(**FLASHBACK:** the smashing of your little head trying to ram through a circle the size of a doughnut hole.) A newborn cries not because she's in shock at having been ripped out of her cozy amniotic fluid and thrust unforgivingly into the rawness of foreign air— she does so because she's screaming her first words of protest: *"What the fuck is this, and why do I have the headache from Hell?"*

But if you're me and manage to get yourself conceived by a crazy woman from the ghetto who is steppin' out with a married man, then you may just end up entering this planet via an ignoble birth that has you doing a slip-n-slide into a toilet in 1948 in the heart of the ghetto in Cleveland, Ohio. And much to the delight of the village gossips, your birth will remain fodder for their front-stoop clacking for years to come, but your first words will be guaranteed to be ones of ferocious protest against the gods: *"Shit, shit, shit, shit, shit—how the hell did I end up here?"*

❋❋

"There goes dat bastard child of dat heffa, Georgia. You know, the woman on the corner who's bat-shit crazy and hangs out on Cedar Avenue screamin' at everybody about the 'Russians are comin'—the Russians are comin'?' She the one done tol' me dat she had a tumor when she started gettin' fat years ago for no account. Um, hum—tumor my ass. Heard dat 'tumor' dropped into the toilet ten years ago when Crazy-woman's ass exploded with gas, and 'Little Miss Tumor' started hollerin' and screamin' for dear life—some say you could hear dat chil' all the way to Cincinnati. Georgia done name dat toilet-bowl deposit after President Roosevelt's wife. Can you believe dat shit? Wonder who she thinks her bastard gonna be first lady of: The Turd Kingdom?"

What is worse than being born in a toilet is being born in the segregated East Side of Cleveland and believing, until I was ten years old, that I (a) had a father who loved me dearly (apparently, a hero who was away at sea keeping America safe), (b) was born in an all-white hospital while everyone fawned over my birth because I was such a beautiful baby, and (c) had a white doctor so enamored by me that he named me after his woman and a former president's wife: *Eleanor Lois.* When you're the offspring of a crazy woman, it can sometimes take eons to find out the truth about who you are, which sure makes it hard to know where you're going in life. It wasn't until I was ten years old that a woman who I thought was my "Aunt Bernice" but turned out to be my half-sister, was more than happy to tell me—in one massive run-on sentence that she spit out in ten seconds flat—the low-down about my sorry-ass life.

*"FOOL-what-do-you-mean-<u>you</u>-were-born-in-that-'Whites-Only'-St.-Luke's-Hospital-and-was-so-special-the-white-doctor-named-you-after-that-ugly-ol'-white-woman-who-used-to-be-America's-first-lady-when-**I-know-for-a-fact**-YOU-WAS-BORN-IN-A-TOILET, and-I-should-know-'cause-I'm-your-half-sister-and-I-was-there-when-you-came-out-of-Mama's-peepee-hole-and-you-sho'-didn't-remind-nobody-of-no-rich-white-man's-first-lady!"*

"And-another-thing: your-sorry-ass-daddy-ain't-no-navy-man-out-at-sea, he-is-a-goddamn-mailman-who-lives-three-streets-over-with-a-wife-and-four-kids-so-stop-actin'-like-you-a-somebody-when-you-is-a-nobody-like-the-rest-of-us."

This kind of comeuppance would gnaw at me all of my life—as if it were a dog chewing on a favorite bone. Throughout the years, I'd brag about some innocuous something or other ("I got an 'A' on the test; I got an 'A' everybody!"), and somebody I hardly knew would derive great pleasure in letting me and all people groups within a hundred mile radius know that *everybody in the class* got an 'A' simply for showing up that day—making me nobody special. It was the teacher's way of encouraging class attendance in a ghetto school where learning was an afterthought to poverty, neglect, and indifference.

It shouldn't have taken me until I was ten years old to know that the stories my mother wove about my existence and hers were fantasies. If I had been paying attention, I would have stopped to analyze my earliest memories, which were like flash bulbs trying to get me to pay attention to the snapshots of incongruity chronicling my life.

SNAP! My first memory is as a four-year-old, and it features a crystal-clear image of my mother and three significant items that inform the memories to come: a tiny Christmas tree about the size of my toddler height with a star made out of black-and-white news-paper, a photo on the mantle of a laughing image of me as a baby in a pink dress and a big white bow, and a white metal toy table decorated in Mickey and Minnie Mouse characters with porcelain cups and saucers resting on top. The table plays a tune when I open the drawer to it, and it makes my mother laugh every time I do it. This mother of my four-year-old memory is magnificently beautiful and luminous as only a child can remember about his or her mother. Photographs would later confirm my remembrance of a mocha-chocolate slender woman with big tits, an up-do hairstyle (a Betty Grable/Lucille Ball contribu-tion of the day), bright red lips, and a smile that could melt an iceberg. The thing that strikes me the most about this memory and why I think it crystalized in my brain is because it was the first and last time I ever remember hearing my mother laugh, the first and last time I remember her hugging me or playing with me *("How old is my precious baby?"—"I four years old, I four, Mama!"—"That's right! Come give Mama a big hug, Sweetie-pie")*, and the first and last time I remember ever being happy in my mother's presence.

SNAP! The second memory of my childhood must have been shortly after the Christmas scene, because I am on a bus rumbling through city streets, squatting on my knees, and looking out the window at the mounds of snow with discarded Christmas trees on top of them that had been left by the side of the road. I don't remember leaving the bus, but I do remember ending up in a kitchen that is all white (white floors, white counters, white appliances) and sitting at a white kitchen table while a white woman in a white dress yells at my mother and wags her finger in Mama's face. My mother is holding a baby in her lap, and this is the first time that it registers in my brain that this baby is part of my family. I can't remember my mother being pregnant, the baby being born, or what the baby's name is. I just remember noting that the baby is the blackest person I've ever seen and how my family is the only color in the room. What little hair the baby has looks like patches of fuzz on a peach, and she is wearing a pink dress identical to the outfit I wore in my smiling picture on the mantle. "Charcoal Baby" has the biggest eyes—like Tweety Bird—and she incessantly sucks her thumb as if keeping that appendage firmly entrenched in her mouth depends on us not being swallowed up by the scary white woman.

The white lady yells at my mother for the longest time while Mama stares at the white ceiling as if she were looking for something in the white light fixture that could help us escape.

"Georgia, we had an understanding that your maid's job was a live-in position. You can't work for me taking care of my home and my children while taking care of your own children at the same time. Find someone out there to take care of your picaninnies so

that you can do your job properly—if not, I have no choice but to let you go!"

As we leave the house and make our way back to the bus stop, I remember being afraid but not understanding why. Mama isn't smiling, she isn't talking, and she just stares straight ahead. Sometime during the long walk, I come to my first flawed deductive reasoning about life as I pull at my mother's dark brown coat to ask her about my toddler epiphany— *"Mama, you think the white lady's house is why we calls them 'The White People' and us 'The Colors People'?"*

SNAP! The last image that forms the trifecta memory of my four-year-old existence is when I encounter a train of words that I'd never heard before but end up rocking my world anyway: *goddamn, son-of-a-bitch,* and *evicted.* On a cold, winter's night sometime shortly after the white house excursion, Mama, Charcoal Baby, and I come upon the scene of our apartment duplex sporting a padlock and a sign with big letters on the door that some of the neighbors are pointing to and talking about as they stare at us coming down the street. Other people are running off with our furniture and clothes that have been thrown out on the snow mound along with our Christmas tree, but no one has taken the baby picture of me smiling in my pink dress (the picture glass now broken in pieces) on top of the trash heap. I hear the tinkling sound of my mangled toy table as the scavengers drop and crush my tea set when they scurry away in the dark. Lots of people stand around and point at us, but no one offers to help, and I overhear one of them say: *"Evicted at Christmastime with yo' kids in the middle of the night—now that's some cold-ass shit."*

※❀※

I don't remember much about that night following the eviction except that we walked for a very long time while Mama cried and cursed the night: *"goddamn, son-of-a-bitch —how could you evict me and my babies at Christmas time?"* We eventually knocked on a door of a house I'd never seen before. A woman let us in and led us to a room with one bed, and we all climbed into that same bed. It had a urine-stained mattress, no sheets, and millions of horrid little creatures called bedbugs that ate us alive and exploded with blood when you squeezed them. But Charcoal Baby and I plastered ourselves against Mama's body and instantly fell asleep to the white noise of her sobs—just happy to stop walking. Years later, I would overhear the pastor's wife of a still very prominent black church in Cleveland gossiping about that *"Maxwell woman and her two bastard children"*—how she had *"wandered the streets all night after being evicted by her white landlord, 'cause she didn't have a husband and couldn't keep a job."* The pastor's wife and the deacons' wives sprinkled their gossip with liberal doses of moral clucking as they summarily passed judgment on my Mama.

"Georgia probably would have let them chillrens freeze to death if it hadn't been for that low-life Maxine takin' pity on them in the middle of the night and givin' them a place to live in her boardin' house. Course they might have been better off freezin' to death than holed up in that den of iniquity. Ain't no accountin' for the trash that frequented that place on any given Saturday night—um, um, um!"

❋❋

I am discovering that the system—where anyone who has a vagina has the potential to get pregnant and have an innocent baby—needs a major overhaul. What was God thinking when he set up the whole one-eyed snake and muffin duet and gave it an automatic baby-forming mechanism without qualifications? It isn't the people who have the power to copulate who should be able to abort a baby, but vice versa, because maybe vulnerable children would have more of a fighting chance at survival once they started trying to make their way on Earth if they could have some say about who their parents would be. Sometime before the end of the fourth week when the human baby is about the size of a poppy seed and preparing to compete in the in vitro Miss Toad Pageant, the baby should get a missive from Command Central that says:

SELF-ABORT, SELF-ABORT!

"You are the culmination of a paranoid-schizophrenic woman and a low-life, married man who got drunk one night and did 'the wild thing.' The foolish woman who is your mother thinks she's in love because she'll believe anything a man tells her, but the man she hooked up with is a booty-chaser of the nth degree. When you meet him, you will despise him. No good thing can come out of this DNA cocktail—trust me! Open up the escape hatch and summarily reject both of your parents—forewarned is forearmed!"

If only. Instead, every baby enters the world at the behest of a sperm that can swim and an egg that can't get out of its own way, and hopes for the best with no guarantees. Even if the mother and father are the bee's knees and the baby is born in the best of circumstances, he or she can still turn out to be a serial killer, and the baby of the crazy woman and the asshole can turn out to be clear-eyed, sane, talented, smart, and spiritually strong. It's an age-old mystery that only something much bigger than a Big Bang Theory can explain in the end.

2

The Royal House Of Queen Maxine

"QUEEN (n): A woman by whom the realm is ruled when there is a king, and through whom it is ruled when there is not."
— Ambrose Gwinnett Bierce

Do you know what I've discovered about getting shipwrecked on your journey through life? It's best to know the type of government that rules the "country" where you get stranded. It will save you a lot of heartache if you know the lay of the land, how many multi-headed monsters have sanction there, and maybe—just maybe—you won't end up being eaten by a Scylla knockoff.

⁂

"Elnora! ELNOOOOOOOORA! Where the hell is you, you little nigga'? When The Queen calls you,

you better come. Don't you hide from us, chil'. Get yo' lil' raggedy lard-ass on up here soz we can tear it up. And while you're at it, bring us some of that bar soap soz we can wash yo' fuckin' mouth out wit it.

"If we done tol' you once, we done tol' you a thousand times that <u>you jest five years old</u>, and you gots no right to be usin' the Lord's name in vain and callin' people assholes. Yo' Mama don't seem to be payin' no 'tention to the fact that you turnin' into a lil' heathen, so we guess we gots to take matters into our own hands.

"STOP WIGGLIN' or else you'll really get the shit beat outta you! It's yo' lucky day that we knows Jesus or we'd really give you somethin' to cry about—now shut the fuck up!"

When it comes to having one's butt thrashed almost every single day for this or that infraction against a queen of a ghetto mansion, even a little kid can figure out ways to survive her wrath. Also, a reign of terror on one's ass can cause the memory of a child—especially a five-year-old child—to sharpen and crystalize about the people who once ruled there and all its outrageous inhabitants.

❋❂❋

The boarding house that Mama, Charcoal Baby, and I landed in on the night of the eviction was run by a black woman known by its inhabitants as Queen Maxine. (There was no "Mr. Queen Maxine.") We had lived there for a year before my child's mind could basically comprehend just who or what our landlady was up to as the ruler of our domain and how I was supposed to survive her. Queen Maxine was a chain-smoking, whiskey-drinking, church going, ghetto entrepreneur in her early thirties who had migrated from Alabama to Cleveland as a teenager. The Queen and hundreds of thousands of other Black folks from the South had fled segregation, lynching, and poverty in their southern home states over the course of a ten-year period— hopping on the Northern Gravy Train looking for a better life in the Promised Land of factories and better pay in Cleveland, Detroit, and Chicago. Like so many others, Queen Maxine never found the life of "milk and honey" that was promised in her new home because of its systematic segregation, and she learned to make do in order to survive. As hard-ass as the Queen seemed, she had one redeeming quality: she never hesitated to take in strays when they washed up on her shores.

The dirt-encrusted, rat-infested, roach-inundated building that The Queen governed had once been inhabited by white immigrants who fled to the West Side of Cleveland once they got "two nickels to rub together," as the old folks used to say. The immigrants would leave behind the slum landlords who greeted the Negroes flooding in from the South with chopped-up housing units, exorbitant rents, inadequate sanitation, and bottomed-out property values. The Queen's house should have been demolished long before we moved there. It had holes in the roof, sagged in the middle, leaned in the front, and buckled in the back. Every papered wall was covered with years of soot from the coal-burning furnace that had married with the cloying grease of fried food and boiled chittlins (hog guts) that made the wall-paper design almost indiscernible. *Were those flowers or chubby demons trying to escape and run for the hills—who could tell?* In an attempt to cover up a couple of really prominent stains—perhaps the obliterated innards of a squished cockroach or two— someone had tacked up two pictures whose presence mocked and taunted the inhabitants on a daily basis. A copy of an Ansel Adams' photograph seduced the renters with a Wild West landscape as it looked down upon the occupants who would probably never leave the crowded alleyways of Central Avenue—let alone explore the wide-open spaces of the Rocky Mountains. Salvation proved even more elusive through a calendar page of a classic picture of "white Jesus" covering up the other splat, that was more of a silent witness to the entrapment of the souls of the residents—rather than a possible road to their redemption.

A cast of characters right out of CCC (Colored Central Casting) was the lifeblood at The Queen's. There was **Policy Rufus** (a numbers runner), **Slick Willie** (thief extraordinaire), **Nasty-ass Chester** (the resident molester), **Foxy Clarisse** (a prostitute), **Cadillac Marshall** (Clarisse's pimp), **Aunt Sukey** (the blind-in-one-eye, wheelchair bound, self-proclaimed "little-ass-tearer-upper"), and **Crazy-ass Mama Maxwell** (my soon-to-be-revealed paranoid-schizophrenic mother). Even Charcoal Baby and I were anointed with names more befitting our environs by the inhabitants. Charcoal Baby was dubbed **"Pee-wee"** shortly after our arrival because malnutrition, chronic sickness, filth, and general neglect had stunted her growth. I was crowned with the name **"Lil Lard-ass Pipsqueak"** because I never stopped eating and I never stopped talking—as if scarfing down any available bit of food that wasn't crawling and talking a mile a minute could make me larger than life and help me conquer my surroundings. All these people with their perfect monikers—looking as if they were auditioning for a blacksploitation movie—came to Queen Maxine's kitchen beauty parlor every Saturday morning to have their hair straightened, conked, waved, curled, and cut in the style of the day by The Queen (one of hundreds of Cleveland's kitchen beauticians).

❋❋

Maxine's establishment was a clearing house for making money in any shape, form, or fashion that a hustler could imagine. Under The Queen's roof, the local prostitute (Foxy Clarisse) could get her hair washed in the same sink as the stolen pig guts got cleaned in by the residents' new five-year-old sous chef. The Saturday night party would be held in Queen Maxine's living room (reasonable cover charge expected). Said prostitute could attend Maxine's house party dressed to the nines in a stolen outfit (down to the perfect size and color) that had been hand-delivered that morning by Slick Willie during her bi-weekly hair appointment. Miss Foxy Clarisse could pay for the purchase of her top-drawer outfit with the money she made plying her trade, or if she was lucky, from the money Policy Rufus would pay out for her numbers win. Miss Clarisse would hope for the windfall that everybody in the ghetto did from their numbers bet (the illegal precursor to the lottery) because that would mean "her ship had come in," and along with her new outfit she could purchase a one-way ticket out of the Hell-hole that I would come to know as home.

✳✳✳

Slick was one of the stock players who never failed to appear every Saturday morning. If there had been a black **GQ** magazine in 1953, Slick Willie (built like a mocha-colored Fred Astaire with a 100-watt smile), would have been its favorite cover model. Slick even moved through life with a dancer's agility and a game show host's flair. Dressed to the nines and sporting a hat that was always cocked over his right eye, Slick would burst through the door as if being pushed by a gale-force wind off of Lake Erie as he lugged boxes of hot goods into Queen Maxine's living room and worked his sales pitch on a captive audience, never once slowing down, as he delivered his customers' orders.

"POLICY! How's it hangin' my man? I got those neckties you was eyein' in Higbee's department sto' the other day. I gots you one in blue <u>and</u> one in brown—soz you'd have a choice, 'cause I know how sportin' you always like to be. And look-a-here: I'll gives you a deal—two for the price of one, cause you my main man!

"Hey, Foxy-Mama, what you doin' up in here on this Saturday mornin'? Don't you get yo' hair done next week? Well, never you mind. Cause yo' red satin dress 'fell of the truck' early on its way to Halles Bros, and it's in a size ten just like you wanted. For a little extra, I'll throw in matchin' earrings. They'll look mighty fine on you—that's for sho'. Don't tell me ol' Slick don't take good care of his best customers. Oh, Lordie—yes I do!

"Mama Maxwell, how you doin', Baby? I hear you don't get out much atal no mo'. Them chillren of yours look like they could use some new clothes. Every time I see 'em, they is half naked. I got some things in the trunk of my car that should be just about they size. You can pay me next time if you're short on cash. You know that now, don't you? Any friend of Maxine's is a friend of mine.

"And BE-AU-TY Queen Maxine—hey Darlin'! I could smell your cookin' all the way across town. How about a plate of some of dem chitlins you got on the stove for the party tonight? And while you at it, lay on me a helpin' of greens and some cornbread, Queenie Baby, if you please, 'cause you cook almost as good as you conk my do."

I lived at Maxine's until I was eight years old and during that time Pee-wee and I saw everything from cigarettes to TV's ordered and sold in that house. Today's Zappos and QVC have nothing on Slick Willie. Because of Slick, Queen Maxine would be one of the first people in our neighborhood to own a black and white TV and a washing machine with automatic rollers that could devour a small child if she got too close to it when it was wringing out clothes.

✺❂✺

Not that anyone was ever paying much attention to my well-being as a child in the "if you want it, come and get it" atmosphere that was my new home, but even if they had been, there wasn't a door that could keep me locked in or out. Even as a five-year-old, I'd be seen running the streets in the summer time as the sun was coming up. When I was six years old, I snuck into the backdoor of a neighborhood store and stole as much grape and cherry pop a little red wagon could hold and be hauled into hiding by a little chubby half-pint of a kid. Word went out throughout the neighborhood that Mr. Gillespie's store had been robbed, and a "chubby-ass little colored gal" was seen high-tailing it down an alleyway at breakneck speed with a wagon load of contraband. Queen Maxine knew it could only be one person. To keep from getting caught, I had to bury the pop bottles all over the communal backyard and underneath various neighbors' back porches (they're probably still there today). For six months, The Queen, randomly and without warning, initiated a Nazi, military search and seizure operation on my mouth (*"Open up yo' mouth and stick out yo' tongue, you lil' shit, 'cause if we sees one trace of purple or red on yo' tongue, we gonna tear up yo' ass so bad that you gonna turn from black to white—you hear what I'm sayin,' you lil' hooligan?"*). It is to my credit as a first-class, pint-sized thief and to The Queen's stupidity that the pop was never found, but I also could never risk drinking it or bragging about my heist, so maybe The Queen was smarter than I thought.

※❈※

I know I was a terror. No one spoke of being ADD/ADHD in the ghetto then. You were either crazy or you weren't. I guess I was a little bit crazy. I also know that everyone preferred my sister, Pee-wee, over me because she said about five words every fifth month and constantly hid to make herself remain out of sight and thus, out of mind. My sister would go into hiding whenever something frightened her—*which was usually everything.* Pee-wee was the spitting image of the original Buckwheat in the "The Little Rascals," except she never smiled and her eyes seemed to be twice the size of the character actor. At the slightest provocation—a simple "boo" uttered by me from out of a shadowy corner—Pee-wee's little face would disappear as her eyes would flair open, melding together to almost look like one large white orb as she let loose a three-staccato scream: *"EEK-EEK-EEK!"* As a follow-up act, urine would turbo-charge out of every opening of her droopy, cloth-diapered butt, soaking everything and everyone within a three-foot radius.

My sister rarely talked the first five years of her life because to talk got you noticed in that mad-house and to be noticed got you beat by whatever was at hand—switch cut from a tree, a razor strop, or a belt. Pee-wee figured out at an early age that the way to survive Queen Maxine was to hide in the shadows and let my motor-mouth draw all the fire. Refusing to come out of the shadows made my sister, Pee-wee, a target of my hyper-activity, and surviving me would be a miracle.

"Pee-wee, stick your finger in that trap. See if it can catch a rat—why don't you," I'd suggest, as we would pass by a multitude of traps lined up like rail cars waiting for rodent passengers. *"Psst, Baby, don't you want to eat this delicious banana-leaf mud pie I made, just for you?"* I'd ask, as I cooked it over a pit I'd built in the backyard, replete with fire and an old frying pan. When I couldn't get Pee-wee to eat fried dirt or use her fingers as stand-ins for a rodent in a rat trap, I once tied a sheet around her two-year-old body and wildly swung her back and forth over the pavement below from a second-floor balcony. She was saved by a neighbor who, seeing a wide-eyed baby screaming one long "EEEEEEEEEEEK" as she flew past his living room window a couple of times like a pendulum, had the where-with-all to grab Pee-wee in mid-swing on the third pass and drag her to safety over his balcony wall. No less than a week later, I enticed my sister to climb into a large box so that I could give her a roller coaster ride down a long flight of curved wooden stairs (rendering her temporarily unconscious). These scenes were always followed by the Queen frantically resuscitating the vomiting, flattened, or unconscious Pee-wee while screaming at the top of her queenly lungs,

"ELNOOOOOOORA! YOU LIL DEMON! YOU BETTER HOPE JESUS COMES BACK BEFO' WE GETS HOLD OF YO' ASS—'CAUSE, SOON AS WE BRINGS PEE-WEE BACK TO LIFE, YOU IS ONE DEAD CHUBBY-ASS LIL MUTHAFUCKA!"

I could never tell whether Queen Maxine's commandeering of me as a sous chef of chittlin' cleaning at five years old was punishment for the torture of Pee-wee or a reenactment of the 9th level of Dante's Inferno. The Queen did have a flare for the dramatic. Surely no sulfuric smell from Hell could outmatch the smell of raw hog guts or be more punishing. I was forced to clean buckets of chitlins with a paring knife that was so sharp it could slice the tip of a finger off with the slightest misstep. I had to remove the membrane of the chittlins, and then I had to rub my fingers up and down the insides of the greasy white tubes to remove fecal matter and debris. It would take days for the pervasive odor of bile to leave my nostrils, and to this day I can't stomach the smell of raw pork. I am convinced that the walls of Hell are lined with pig intestines.

Trying to escape the chore of cleaning hog guts is one of the reasons I started slipping out of the house and running the streets at all hours of the night and day as a little kid. Being the ubiquitous little urchin who was constantly zipping in and out of alleyways would get me my first paying gig, at the age of six years old, working for the Mafia as a little bag girl collecting bets and dropping them off at the collection site in my neighborhood.

※※

I am discovering if I were the god who had created those people that got duped by a snake, one of the things I would have done is furnish music tracks for my peeps after I kicked them out of my garden for disobeying my rules. This way even a five-year-old child, thousands or millions of years later (depending on one's frame of reference), would know to run for her life if she heard something similar to the "Jaws" theme song. On the other hand, if she heard Bobby McFerrin's "Don't Worry, Be Happy" song, she'd know that the smell of chitlins was as bad as it was going to get *sans* garden, and she could just chill out and try not to inhale. But white Jesus was hanging on the wall in the calendar picture—and he heard and saw it all— and never breathed a mumbling word. If I were a god that wanted my creation to believe in me when they were wallowing in the smell of hog guts, roaches, rats, neglect, and poverty, I would have looked down from the wall calendar at the Queen's house and given that little five-year-old some kind of clue that he was available for rescue missions or amenable to a warning shout-out, *"Psst! You in danger, Baby!"*

3

Two Truths And A Lie

"I'm not upset that you lied to me, I'm upset that from now on I can't believe you."—
Friedrich Nietzsche

Do you know what I've discovered about growing up as a poor, black child in The Cleve in the 50s? There were monsters here, there, and everywhere: childhood monsters under my bed, movie monsters in my head, and human monsters I'd come to dread—ready to make their debut when the time was ripe. But there was one difference between the movie monsters and the human monsters: you always knew who the big screen monsters were, but you could never tell what kind of monsters were hiding inside the hearts and minds of the humanoids.

"Pee-wee, the Boogey Man is the really scary thing dat lives in the basement and eats bad little kids in the night," I said as I relayed my six-year-old monster dissertation to my three-year-old sister. "He works for Aunt Sukey; that's why she always sayin' if we ain't good she gonna have The Boogey tear our asses up. She say even though she blind in one eye, The Boogey got eyes in the back of his head and he can see everythin' we do—even when she can't. I mean, I don't know bout you, but dat scares the shit outta me—you know what I mean? Hey baby, wake up! You keep fallin' asleep, and I gots to tell you something important if you don't plan on gettin' gobbled up like a chicken wing in this place. You wake?"

"Uh-huh," mumbled the urine-soaked, bed-bug suckled, little urchin known as Pee-wee.

"Okay—pay 'tention. On top of everythin' else, we got the Wolf Man asshole. This monster always starts out lookin' like a white man. I got to tell you, I ain't never seen no Colored man who got turned into a Wolf Man, and I don't know why dat is. I asked The Queen if she know why none of the monsters at the movie be Colored and she say, 'cause 'white folks don't share nothin' with Coloreds—not even dey monsters.' Seems like only white mens have the power to turn into mean old wolves who look like the dogs next door, but for some reason they still keeps dey man legs. The Wolf Man chases after peoples and tears dem into pieces wit his giant teeth when he catches dem."

"Who tol' you dis?" asked the skeptical Pee-wee.

"Me told me dis. I know dis is true 'cause I saw dis wit my own eyes at the Saturday Movie Matinee! See . . . dis is how it goes—the moon makes the monster turn from a white man into a wolf, he starts to grow hair everywhere, and then dat makes him go REALLY CRAZY, 'cause he wants to always be a white man, and he never gave nobody permission to turn him into a wolf."

"How I keep from bein' gobbled up by him, Elno?"

"Dat the easy part. Every time you sees a white man or a full moon, run like a bat outta Hell and hide under the bed until the moon and the white man go away. And while I'm thinkin' about it, I better tell you about Count Dracula. Here you got yourself another damn white man. The Dracula will drink the blood of people until he sucks dem dry, and den he leaves dem lookin' like goddamn raisins. (Dat's why I don't eat fuckin' raisins!) Dracula is the father of all bed bugs, by the way. Of course we gots our Frankenstein, but you can always outrun dat asshole—even with yo' short legs. The only people who can't seem to get out of Frankenstein's way are white villagers, but we lives in Central Avenue and only Coloreds live here.

"Now, the head-cheese of the monster group is the fuckin' Devil and he DOES live where we live. He's the nigga who created ALL monsters, and he tells dem where to go and who to kill. You really gots to watch out for him, Pee-wee, 'cause he'll try and fuck with you every minute of the day."

Thus began my life-long fascination with monsters and the beginning of my monster dictionary—started at six years old and currently open-ended.

❋❖❋

Even as a young child, I could tell that my mother was deteriorating. "Georgia 'Luck' Maxwell" grew old right before my eyes, and she seemed to do so over-night. I didn't realize it then but my forty-four-year-old mother was old by that era's standards to have two little kids. Both Pee-wee and I had been "mistakes" that were the product of a mother who couldn't keep her legs crossed. Almost immediately upon entering Queen Maxine's, my mother had stopped wearing make-up, never dressed in anything but a stained, rag-gedy housecoat and tattered house slippers, and was never without a burning cigarette hanging from the corner of her mouth until the day she died. Mama never went outside except to the backyard to collect the clothes off the line, and her hair turned complete-ly gray as if she were trying to fade away.

When I turned six years old, my mother started talking to "The Invisibles" (The FBI) and the "White Russians" (The KGB). The first time it happened in front of me was when she decided to straighten my hair with a hot comb that had been heated on the gas burner of the kitchen stove. Queen Maxine had quit as my beautician because I had tried to set the house on fire by lining up rolls of toilet paper and tossing lighted matches into the hole of the rolls. Catching me in the act of pyromania was not what caused The Queen's boycott of my nappy head—it was the fact that I refused to show any remorse, or cry when she beat my ass with a razor strop. As she said, "a grown man would have crumbled to his knees at the ass-whupin' I gave that chil' and she didn't even shed a fuckin' tear. What the hell kind of demon-seed did you bring up into my house, Georgia?" Since no self-respecting black person went *au naturel* in those days, Mama had to take over the task of turning my Brillo-type mop into a manageable "do."

I sat on stacks of Sears catalogues on the beauty parlor chair (a.k.a. broke-down kitchentable chair) while inhaling a variety of penny candy I hid in the bib of my proverbial overalls—bought with money I'd stolen from the Queen's purse. I suspected that she knew I often stole a nickel here or a dime there from her purse, but for some reason The Queen turned a blind eye to my thievery. I have no idea why this infraction was given a pass, but it was the one kindness Queen Maxine afforded me as a child—a little candy contraband—the entire time I lived in her house. (When I got greedy and upped the ante to a quarter, all bets were off and my "ass was grass," as she so poetically put it.)

My usually matted hair was combed straight out all over my head, and I looked half-crazed as if I were a prickly ball hanging from a Sweet Gumball Tree in Georgia. While Pee-wee waited for her turn to have her half-dozen strands of hair straightened, she entertained herself by playing finger-soccer with a couple of giant dead roaches on the floor underneath the kitchen table—flicking the roaches into a goalie rat-trap. Her face was covered in a white, thick, smelly cream (as was my mocha-colored face), and her hair resembled a chicken in the process of being plucked—replete with intermittent bald patches throughout her scalp caused by a virulent case of some type of skin disease.

In my mother's attempt to lighten our skin color or maybe even camouflage it, she had performed her version of rudimentary plastic surgery by scrubbing our faces with Clorox bleach and then plastering them with white Noxzema cream. To add insult to injury, Mama had clamped our Portobello noses shut with clothes pins, not to protect us from the noxious bleach and Noxzema smells, but to shape our noses into Doris Day perky sniffers to go along with our skin transformation that Mama hoped would magically morph us from "Colored" to creamy white. It was during one of these beauty routines (black-face-in-reverse) that my mother first explained who the "White Russians" were.

"Nooooooo, I told you I can't do that right now, because the White Russians are monitoring the situation," Mamma hissed out of the left corner of her lips toward the kitchen wall while the cigarette ashes from the right side of her mouth dropped onto my forehead and into my eyes.

"GOBTH DAMMITH WOMAN, DAT FUCKIN' BURNS!" I screamed. The hot straightening comb had fallen onto my scalp at the same time the cigarette ashes landed on my forehead. I tried to breathe through my clamped nose while brushing my fried steaming bangs to the floor. But as my candy slid to the ground and I followed right behind it, my nose clamp popped off and flew into one of the rat traps causing it to slam shut and startling Pee-wee out of her goalie reverie into an "EEK-EEK-EEEK" crescendo that sent her scurrying across the kitchen floor looking for shelter.

"Don't be fresh, and stop your screaming, child, before your loud mouth tips off the White Russians as to my whereabouts," Mama said as she pulled me back into the chair. "I've managed to keep us hidden from them this long, and I can't have you exposing my hideout with your boisterousness."

"Boister what? What fuckin' White Russians, Mama? Where dey at?"

As Georgia slapped me upside the head with her hand while squinting through the cigarette smoke curling up into her nose and eyes, she started to lecture me on the subject I'd heard ever since I first learned to speak. "What did I tell you about minding your grammar? You are a descendent of the Luck family, and we are an upstanding educated people. I will not permit my children to sink to the level of the Negroes in this place. What have I always told you?

'The Lucks pronounce their T's,

We always add our G's,

Prepositions at the end—we never squeeze.

Our "to bes" are always helpers,

Never active or misplaced;

Elocution and penmanship is the

hope of our dark race!'"

"*I'll be damn—is dat all I needs?*" I said. "Then why I got to put up with this fuckin' white shit on my face and scrapin' chitlins for The Queen?"

As Mama utilized her hand as an accent mark upside my head, she started scolding me as if my life depended on understanding her every terrified breath: "I [smack] mean [smack] it [smack], Lard-ass Pipsqueak [double smack]. I have to keep my true identity below the radar and hiding amongst these shiftless Negroes is the perfect disguise. But if my children start talking like them, the FBI won't be able to recognize you, and you won't be rescued when they come to get me."

Mama suddenly started crying and moaning—rocking back and forth—as if she expected the KGB to drop in at any moment to play the numbers and sit down for a dish of chittlins. "Do you want to be left behind in this God-awful place, Eleanor—do you? *Is that what you want?* As soon as I have fulfilled my mission for the government and your daddy's 'ship comes in,' we'll be on our way, but if the White Russians catch me before your Daddy finds us, they will bombard my mind with radar waves and take us captive. God only knows what will happen to you and your sister then. That is why I need to make sure you and Pee-wee get rid of your dark skin and stop talking like the people in this house because we are not from here. Now listen to me and don't forget what I'm telling you in case I get captured: you don't belong here, you are of Cherokee descent which is better than being a Negro, you come from a long line of educated people with money, and we own a farm in Pennsylvania that will offer safe haven—we just need to get back to it before the White Russians catch us. We can't stay here, do you understand me?"

※※

I am discovering that Michael Jackson had nothing on my mother. Before Michael was a squirt in Joe Jackson's thingy, Mama was trying to strip the color off her and her children's faces to erase the pallor of a father she obviously hated but was too delusional to acknowledge. All I know is that from the moment Mama got the memo that skin could be bleached to help one escape one's past, Pee-wee and I were week-ly Noxzema adverts for how to erase a grandfather's African blackness and monstrous ways. In reality there was not enough bleach and Noxzema in the world to eradicate the stain of a father of fourteen children who violated his daughters, slept with every willing woman along his Baptist preacher circuit route, and treated his sons like slaves—causing all of them to flee into obscurity. On the surface, Mama adored the grandfather I never met, but underneath where the Noxzema could not reach, I suspect his actions were the spores that mushroomed into her mental illness. Sometimes families are just not worth the price of admission.

4

When Monsters Come Out To Play

~

"A lot of life is dealing with your curse, deal-
ing with the cards you were given that aren't
so nice. Does it make you into a monster,
or can you temper it in some way, or accept
it and go in some other direction?"—**Wes**
Craven

Do you know what I've discovered about monsters?
There are way too many to keep track of in life. If
in 1954 someone had given me the rundown on
Odysseus' encounter with the Cyclops in Homer's
Odyssey, then I would have recognized Aunt Sukey in
a heartbeat. What looked like a harmless, decrepit,
octogenarian spinster—wheelchair bound, toothless,
blind in one eye from glaucoma, and half blind in the
other eye—was really a ghetto Cyclops who took no
shit from anybody and as my primary caretaker during

the day was the only person I really feared and never talked back to in The Queen's domain. But there has always been a problem with when one gains knowledge about various subject matters—*timing is everything.*

※❦※

Aunt Sukey was The Queen's aunt, head foreman of child labor in the house, and our primary babysitter. Queen Maxine worked during the day—at what, I don't know—but with my mother permanently wed to the wall in any given room, that made Aunt Sukey the next one up to bat to keep an eye on the children. That old woman had been crippled for years, but she could maneuver herself in and around the furniture obstacles with the speed and agility of an Indy 500 driver. With the aid of a wooden cane that she laid across the armrests of her wheelchair, Aunt Sukey would back her wheelchair up into a shadowy corner, bide her time, and wait until one of us (especially me) started getting into things that I shouldn't. Without hesitation, the cane would emerge from a dark corner like a divining rod and snatch, whack, strike, poke, or prod any unsuspecting child within its reach. There was no place I could run or hide that Aunt Sukey wouldn't eventually corner me and beat the shit out of me for some infraction or another. My nickname for Aunt Sukey was "Little-ass-tearer-upper," and she never missed her mark.

By the time I was six years old, I had four jobs—all enforced by Aunt Sukey who was hell-bent on me earning my keep. My first job was cleaning chittlins; my second job was using a broom twice my size to sweep the house whose main source of oxygen seemed to be dirt; my third job was wringing out the laundry we took in for pay; and the fourth job was working as a bag-girl for the numbers runners who shuttled money from semi-private gambling parlors like Queen Maxine's to designated gambling headquarters.

The sweeping job ended up establishing a new form of torture, because rather than scoop up the mountainous piles of dirt that daily seeped into the house, I simply swept them under the throw rugs at various stations around the place. Mama never noticed the six-inch undulating hills of dirt that stopped Aunt Sukey in her tracks, but Queen Maxine discovered them and that was the day she stopped beating me for infractions of the rules and developed "The Mind Fuck."

"Well, Elnora, while you clean up all these piles of dirt, we are gonna take Pee-wee to the Five and Dime and enjoy us some hot dogs and root beer floats. How you like that, you misbehavin' lil ol' devil. Pee-wee, wave bye-bye to yo' juvenile delinquent of a sista. Hmmmm, can't you just taste those hot dogs, Baby? Hmmmmm-um-hmmm! It's a damn shame dat some folks think they can pull one over on The Queen. Some people will never learn, will they Pee-wee?"

The third job Aunt Sukey assigned to me was help-ing Mama as an assistant laundress. My mother didn't have any money because she hadn't worked since the day we landed on Queen Maxine's doorstep. She took in laundry for a fee to help pay for our food. Laundry was a three-step process. The first step involved descending into the unfinished basement where the scary coal furnace and the Boogey Man lived. I know The Boogey lived in the basement because Aunt Sukey told me so—told me more than once that he lay in hiding, waiting to chew up my sorry-ass if I didn't do as I was told. Aunt Sukey forced Mama to take me down into the basement to train me when she did the laundry. I was so afraid of the monsters that lived below the kitchen that during my training sessions I suction-cupped myself to one of Mama's legs and face-planted my cheek to her knees, as if I were Isaac finally catching on that Abraham was up to no good and get-ting ready to sacrifice him at the behest of a seemingly capricious god. No matter how many times I tried to hysterically explain the danger of going into the base-ment to Mama ("DON'T YOU KNOW WOMAN DAT DIS IS THE BOOGEY'S DUNGEON AND HE EATS LITTLE SORRY-ASS KIDS LIKE ME ALIVE?"), it never fazed my mother, and she kept me locked down there until all the clothes were washed and properly wrung out through the automatic rollers on the barrel washing machine. I almost lost my mind from fright.

I was so short for my age that I had to climb up on a wooden packing crate, dig the shirts out of the bottom of the washer while half leaning into the machine and, usually with chubby legs flailing in the air, I would feed the shirts through the wooden rollers that rotated inward while I frantically looked over my shoulder for the approach of The Boogey. My fear of that basement was palpable, and I swear that 'til this day, I can still feel The Boogey's breath on my neck as I imagined he crept closer and closer. Invariably, due to the fear of being gobbled up, I never paid attention to the task at hand of loading the wet laundry in between the rollers, and my fingers would get sucked right into the ringers and get flattened like a pancake. My bloodcurdling screams were always enough to bring some mobile adult—temporarily in their right mind—down into the basement to release my fingers from the demonic washer ringers before any bones were broken. Everyone agreed that a new job needed to be found for me before I completely dismembered myself and ended up being good for nothing.

When Policy Rufus mysteriously disappeared one day, I got pulled from laundry detail and drafted to do the job of being the bag girl that ran the bets to the numbers headquarters that was located in what my child's mind called the "cheese and peanut" shop. I got a job that let me run the streets, got to sidestep the furnace monster, and permanently escape The

Boogey. *Yes, yes, yes!* Who could ask for more? But this was the beginning of a life-long lesson for me that when things look too good to be true, they usually are.

※✖※

With the aid of a giant magnifying glass, Aunt Sukey helped Policy Rufus run his "Nigger Pool," which is what Queen Maxine called the lottery-style numbers racket that was a staple in the East Side of Cleveland in the 50s and 60s. Everybody hoped that their little penny, dime, or dollar bet would pay the next bill or be their ticket out of Hell into the Promised Land. The "Bookie on Wheels" (Aunt Sukey), would arduously log the bets from Queen Maxine's Saturday hair and party customers as she bent over the kitchen table with one cloudy eye plastered to the numbers ledger she kept. Pieces of paper with three digit numbers and bags of money would be given to Policy Rufus by Aunt Sukey, and he would take the numbers slips and money to a headquarters where the main numbers boss would collect everything and pay out what was owed.

As I was barreling between the living room and the kitchen one day, Aunt Sukey—hidden behind the door between the two rooms—slammed her cane across my pathway and trapped me between her and the kitchen table. I immediately ducked underneath her cane and in one fluid motion tried to scamper under the table, out the other end, and through the backdoor to freedom, but Aunt Sukey did a wheelie and raced me to the back of the kitchen—blocking my exit.

"Get! Get yo' lil nappy-head on over to the kitchen table," said Aunt Sukey swinging her cane like a Ninja warrior. "I's got a job for you, and I needs you to obey me in everthin' I tells you about what it is you needs to do."

Although Policy Rufus was Aunt Sukey's numbers' contact, he was just a baby fish in the scheme of things. As time passed, I learned from the gossip at Queen Maxine's that the numbers racket was run by a big-time Colored boss who had murdered a man caught robbing one of his gambling houses. I don't know if my Policy Rufus was the man the big-time boss killed in 1954, all I do know is that one day Policy Rufus was there and the next day he didn't come around anymore, and before I could ask, "What's a bag-girl," I was his six-year-old replacement.

※※

The day I was drafted as the pint-sized numbers runner was just an ordinary day around Central Avenue for me. I got my ass torn up by The Queen for stealing a dollar from her purse and buying a boat-load of penny candy, I terrorized Pee-wee and made her cry, and I paid a neighborhood kid a nickel to give me a ride on the handle bars of his bike to take me halfway to the Cheese Man's shop.

Once the neighborhood kid dropped me off at the corner, I began my scampering between houses, scooting in and out of alleyways, to eventually deliver my numbers bag. Aunt Sukey had pinned the cloth bag inside my shirt under the bib of the overalls so that no one would guess what I was carrying and rob me. I had slipped my proverbial bag of penny candy in-between my bib and my shirt for easy access. My chest looked like the sagging breasts of a seventy-year-old woman, but it served its purpose.

As I was skipping along, sucking on a lollypop, I turned the corner behind the school playground and saw a guy with a stocking cap on his head that I recognized from around the neighborhood. He was bent over a man I'd never seen before and was stabbing him in the chest with an ice pick. I tried to quickly reverse my course, and I almost got away, but the killer grabbed me by the back of my overalls before I could get to the end of the alley. Ice Pick Man picked me up to his eye level and slammed me face first against the brick wall of the school and demanded to know what I had seen. When I replied, "nothin'—just you stabbing that man over there," Ice Pick Man shook me back and forth like a rag doll and said he was going to stab me too for being so nosy. My penny candy stash exploded all over the ground and in the blood puddled around the dead guy's body. At the moment when I should have peed my pants, something in me snapped.

"What the fuck is wrong wit you, muthafucker?" I said as I swung back and forth in the air like a sail that had broken loose from its mast. "Look at what you did to my candy, asshole. You better pick up my shit, or I'll kick yo' ass into next week."

Ice Pick Man looked at me as if I'd lost my mind, and then he started to laugh until he choked as he flung me to the ground next to the dead man. "Damn, you is one crazy-ass little kid. Get on out of here befo' I stab you full of holes like this sorry-ass nigga. And you better not tell a soul what you saw, or I'll come get you, 'cause I know you live at Queen Maxine's with your Mama and your sista. You tell, and I'll kill 'em all when I come to kill you. Matter-o-fact, I think I'll start droppin' by The Queen's ever so often to get my do in shape and check on your ass. How's that suit you, you little mouthy nigga?"

I got out of the alley with as much of my hard-earned candy as I could grab. I forced myself not to cry as I stuffed my precious candy back inside my bib and scrambled out of the alley as fast as I could. I determined never to tell anybody about what I'd seen. I may have been a little kid, but I knew instinctively that Ice Pick Man would keep his threat and stalk me wherever I went. Besides, the killer might have upped the ante when it came to monsters, but I soon forgot about him because the man who took my numbers stash ended up being the monster that beat out all other monsters and kicked my worry about the Ice Pick Man to the back of the line.

✳✳

After I got to the Cheese Man's store and maneuvered my way between barrels of peanuts and rounds of cheese, he led me through a curtain into a backroom. It was a bedroom—big enough for a small bed and a tiny dresser. Aunt Sukey had instructed me to remove my overalls and shirt so the Cheese Man could unpin the money bag where no one who came into the store could see it. So I did as I was told.

I don't remember how long I spent in the backroom of the Cheese Man's store. To this day, I don't remember what he looked like. But I do remember his naked ass and what *it* looked like when he turned his back on me and walked away. I remember he had a mole on his left buttocks. I remember the pain.

✳✳

When I returned to Queen Maxine's, I had no vocabulary to explain what had happened to me. I tried to tell The Queen about my experience with the Cheese Man, but she was watching her daily soap opera, and she didn't bother to look up at me.

"Maxine. . . ."

"Shhhhh! Get out of my face, Elnora—you know you're not allowed to interrupt us when we're watchin' our soaps."

"Maxine, I gotta tell you somethin. . . ."

"Dammit chil'—see what you just did? Now you done gone and caused a distraction when Papa Bauer was finally 'splainin' about the mess his daughter done caused the family. Go down the street and ask Old Lady Morrison what just happened. We gonna be worried sick until we knows every last detail of what's goin' on in that house."

"But Maxine, I need. . ."

"Shut up, chil'; stop all that cryin'! I know you ain't got nothin' to be cryin' about. Go make yourself useful, and gets us a pack of cigarettes at the corner sto' while you at it."

I ran to find Mama, but she was doing her obligatory communing with the wall. When I tried to tell her about the Cheese Man, she asked me the one defining question of my precarious existence: "Who are you, and who sent you here?"

As I started to whimper and cry, I said, "Mama, the Cheese Man hurt me."

"I can't talk to you," she said, as she ran away from me toward the stairs, trying to escape me and my words. "You are here to trap me. I know their tricks. They'll try anything."

"But Mama it's me, Eleanor . . . ."

For just a moment my mother hesitated as a flicker of reality tried to break in on her preferred world, and a flash of horror born out of realization skirted across her face. But just as quickly, the awakening vanished. "I don't believe that for a minute," she snapped. "How do I know you're not a Russian spy sent here to destroy me?"

I had no answer for my mother that day or all the other days after that that the Cheese Man continued to mess with me. Even though I told Aunt Sukey what happened to me, she sent me back over and over again with her bags of cash and bets trying to win her ticket to Paradise. The extent of her one-eyed compassion was to say, "You better stop yo' lyin' chil' or The Boogey Man really will come and git you when you sleep. Jesus don't like lyin' lil chilrin."

❈❈

I am discovering that when a child is abused she will spend the rest of her life trying to get someone to listen to her story—to believe her—to tell her that she's going to be okay and a monster attack or twenty won't define her forever. But to not be heard—to not be believed—to not be vindicated when attacked by monsters is the cruelest of all fates because it leaves a child angry, rudderless, and ashamed. It was an ordinary day in a poor, black child's neighborhood, but because no one would listen to my story, abuse became what I grew accustomed to on any given day—it became ordinary. The question that I pondered for years afterwards would be: will this make me a monster, too?

5

Better The Devil(S) You Know

~

*"It takes ten times as long to put yourself
back together as it does to fall apart."*—
Mockingjay/The Hunger Games, by
Suzanne Collins

Do you know what I've discovered about hospitality?
The warranty on the welcome mat is extremely tenuous and short lived—especially when the houseguest begins to feel entitled to the generosity of the provider.

※※

Almost four years to the day after we stumbled into The Queen's house, she kicked us out. Queen Maxine got into an argument with Mama while we were eating lunch. Mama complained that she hated eating Colored people's food of chitlins, chicken wings, collard greens, rice, beans, and liver and onions all the time. My mother told The Queen that she would have to serve better cuisine if she expected Mama to continue to let The Queen have the pleasure of her company.

"I need a better quality of food to be able to strategize against my enemies—I thought I had made that perfectly clear, Maxine," lectured my mother as if she were the Queen of England. At which point, the only queen within thousands of miles told Mama to get off her "fat ass and get a job and maybe the cuisine would then come up to Her Highness' standards."

Pee-wee and I sat at the kitchen table eating our delicious chicken wings and rice and followed this verbal volley back and forth with our eyes for another five minutes or so—knowing better than to utter a goddamn peep, if we knew what was good for us. Besides, we had no complaints; we loved The Queen's cooking.

Mama served her next verbal shot in her best Scarlett O'Hara voice: "Why should I work to pay you for anything? You have a job, which is sufficient for all of us. Besides, I have more important things to do than to lower myself to the menial labor for which you seem to be so well suited."

The Queen: Deuce.

Crazy woman with a death wish: Deuce.

Before Pee-wee and I could blink, The Queen gained two points and won the match when she pulled out a gun from her purse and threatened to blow Mama's "goddamn ass into next week." After Slick

Willie and one of his friends wrestled the gun from The Queen, they talked her into leaving with them so that she could cool down. Queen Maxine took their advice but only after she served my mother a parting shot: "You better not be here when we get back, bitch! You and your nasty-ass kids better get the hell out of my house, or we'll put a bullet through your fuckin' head, and we means it this time."

※❀

I will never know how Mama found the one-room basement apartment we ended up inhabiting on such short notice. What is really strange about my third home is that I have conflicting memories about its quality in the reruns of my dreams and nightmares. The conflict depends on which memory (of the only three I have retained), comes to mind: *The Homecoming, The Enemy Within, or The Invasion.*

※❀

On the day I met my father for the first time, the basement apartment seemed to have a beautiful hue to it—perfect for a homecoming. Sunlight was streaming through the small window above the kitchen table, and it gave everything and everybody in the dwelling a deep, rich glow as if we were in the opening scene of a Fred Astaire and Ginger Rogers' movie.

In the beginning, the apartment seemed warm and secure even though our bed was a mattress on the floor in the corner of the kitchen, covered by a smelly, stained blanket. Mama was confident that the White Russians couldn't find us there. She was sure they had discovered our previous hide-out and were the ones who had messed with Queen Maxine's brain which caused her to try and assassinate Mama.

We hadn't been in the new place for more than a few weeks when Mama started to seem almost normal. One day, as Mama tidied up the apartment, she told us that a very special man was coming soon. She cautioned us that we were to be on our best behavior because she *really* wanted him to like us, and if he did, he'd take us all home with him.

When Pee-wee and I talked about the transformation of our mother who had curled her hair, put on some makeup and a pair of high heels and a dress we'd never seen before, we knew exactly what was happening. We were Shirley Temple fans, after all, and we'd seen the *The Little Princess* at least three times. It was our favorite movie and we knew the ending as well as we knew the back of our hands: *child of unfortunate circumstances finds her father (a soldier who has suffered temporary amnesia), regains all her family riches, goes to live with her father, and lives happily ever after!*

Our father was coming home.

When I was a little girl, I once saw another Shirley Temple movie where she saw her father coming from afar, and as he drew near, she ran towards him and threw herself into his arms. (It might have been a kind uncle; the relationship was inconsequential to me—it was a man who was a protector of young girls.) As they swirled and danced together, he had the most inviting and enveloping smile of love that just broke my heart. It was mesmerizing, and this was the scene I decided would be the appropriate one for greeting the man who would finally reveal himself as my daddy.

The day my father was due to arrive, my mother couldn't sit still. She started to whistle. On most days she was a zombie, not moving or talking for hours on end unless she was engaged in conversation with the wall. But that day she was all aflutter, whistling as she moved from corner to corner—a school girl waiting for her first date to knock on the door. I should have remembered the folklore she'd admonished me with all my life: "Whistling girls and crowing hens, always come to some bad end."

Pee-wee and I were ready and waiting. Pee-wee sat on the floor with her back against the far wall opposite the bottom of the stars. She was in a safe position but able to catch a clear view of our father when he opened the door. My sister was all dressed up with a huge white bow attached to the lone braid on top of her head and a pink hand-me-down dress that was three sizes too big for her. I had on my best overalls and a white blouse on my head to simulate Shirley Temple's hair—topped with one of Mama's old black "Sunday-go-to-meeting hats" to keep my "blonde hair" in place. At such short notice, I had not been able to figure out how to make ringlets out of my blouse-hair, but I figured this would have to do. Mama kept trying to pull the blouse off my head, but I resisted so tenaciously that she finally gave up and went back to fretting over her own hairdo.

At my mother's herald of *"He's coming children; I can hear him coming—straighten up and fly right,"* I nervously took up a squatting position on the edge of the landing beside the door at the top of the stairs. I must have resembled a chubby, chocolate gargoyle intent on warding off any evil spirits that would interfere with me finally meeting my father. When the door opened, my plan was to shout, "FAATHA," in my best "white-girl voice" to get his attention. Assuming he would turn and look for the endearing voice that had called his name, I hoped to do a perfect swan dive into my father's long lost arms as my "hair" flowed languidly across my shoulders in the breeze. In my imagination, my affectionate father would playfully pretend to almost stumble down the stairs, but then he would steady himself while he enveloped me in his strong arms and merrily laughed at the beautiful darling I had become while he had been away.

As in most moments in life that are overly fantasized, this one did not live up to the movie in my head. I had miscalculated the angle and timing of my father's entry (I hadn't counted on him having his own key and moving so quickly). The delicate leap I had imagined turned into a time-delayed attack-dog stranglehold around the back of his neck when I dove toward him. I landed on his back when he was half-way down the stairs and frantically wrapped my arms around his windpipe to keep from falling. My "hair" swung around and smacked him in the face. This caused him to miss a step. In retaliation, his left arm swiftly struck out against my body as I frantically clung to his neck. The force of his blow slammed me hard against the wall—even so, I screamed out: *"FAATHA!"* The man who had impregnated my mother screamed: *"WHAT THE FUCK IS THIS? GET OFF ME, YOU LIL' SHIT!"*

As he brushed past me, I noticed he had on pants with a stripe on the side and wore a cap with some sort of visor that confirmed in my childish imagination that he was a soldier of some sort—just like Shirley's father. It never occurred to me that his clothing could be the uniform of a ghetto mailman.

❋❖❋

After the demise of our long held fantasy we presented a sorry tableau of misery: one furious male stranger, one screaming banshee of a mother, one whimpering, bruised, and humiliated eight year old, and one traumatized five year old who had peed right through her diaper as she announced her vocal assessment of the entire pathetic scene: *"EEK, EEK, EEEEEEEK."*

Just like that, the apparition of my father was gone and the only indicator that he was ever there was a small pile of crumbled dollar bills he had thrown at Mama as the door slammed behind him. Other than dismissing me as if he were swatting a fly, he never acknowledged his children's presence that day or any day afterwards. He must have been the one who had gotten us the apartment because he had a key, but he never used the key again. After that encounter, my mother permanently crossed over to the catatonic state in the "land of the wall." She didn't feed us, she didn't talk to us, and she didn't bathe or dress us. We just didn't exist. It was our need to survive that prompted the neighbors to call Child Services when Pee-wee and I were caught stealing food from the neighborhood garbage cans and voraciously devouring it as if we were feral cats.

✳✳

"Mrs. Maxwell, my name is Sally Perkins and I am a social worker with the Cuyahoga County Department of Human Services. May I sit down?"

(No answer.)

"Mrs. Maxwell, my records show that Eleanor was not registered for school until a year after she should have been. At that time, a Mrs. Maxine Brown (it says here, 'of no relation to the child'), signed her up for first grade after being contacted by the authorities. However, the school has indicated that Eleanor's attendance was sporadic and her behavior uncontrollable. According to school records, she used foul language against her first grade teacher and when reprimanded, jumped onto the teacher's lap and urinated on her. The teacher believes the act was vindictive."

(Still no answer as Mrs. Maxwell engaged in what had become her customary rocking back and forth while staring at the wall behind Miss Perkins.)

"Mrs. Maxwell, when the truant officer was sent to Maxine Brown's address, he was told you no longer lived there and had left no forwarding address. It took us months to locate your whereabouts. Why is that, Mrs. Maxwell?"

(No answer—just a barely imperceptible humming was heard from Mrs. Maxwell.)

"Mrs. Maxwell, we were unable to locate you to determine the welfare of your children until one of your neighbors called to report two little girls playing in the street, and one of them matched the description that the truant officer had of Eleanor. Your neighbor said that you usually keep both of the children hidden in this basement, but lately they've been seen escaping through the basement window. The children were reported to be unkempt and emaciated. Both children were seen eating food out of the neighbor-hood garbage cans."

(A recognizable Negro spiritual was heard softly pour-ing out of Mrs. Maxwell's lips as she slowly reached behind her to the kitchen sink: "Soon I will be done wit' de troubles of dis' worl'. . .")

"Mrs. Maxwell, my report also indicates that Eleanor is in need of psychological evaluation. On the last day she was known to attend the first grade, she attacked a sixth grade girl in the street and beat her up so severely that she gave the child a concussion. It took four adults to stop Eleanor from bashing the sixth grader's head into a brick wall. When your daughter was questioned about the incident she showed no remorse and just said that the girl had, and I quote, 'messed with me.' Mrs. Maxwell, I know that you can hear me and I demand that you respond to these allegations."

(A full-throated response bellowed from Mrs. Maxwell's throat: "GOIN' HOME TO MEET MY LORD!")

Pee-wee saw the butcher knife first. It was prob-ably her explosive, standard, monosyllabic "EEK," that saved the white woman from being impaled to the back of the chair. Once she saw what Pee-wee saw, it was certainly Miss Perkins' life flashing before her eyes that jet-propelled her out of her chair, knocking Mama off balance, and thrusting her up the stairs and through the door before Mama could fulfill her secret wish of introducing the social worker to the Devil in person.

Miss Perkins would return but when she did, like any smart white woman going into hostile Negro territory in the 1950s, she'd bring back-up.

※※

Neither Pee-wee nor I have ever been able to explain what happened the night Mama became the "enemy within" and tried to kill me. By now the apartment no longer seemed warm and inviting. After the total abandonment of my father, my environment became crystal clear to me. We were living in a dark, dank room with a tub in the kitchen, one bare light bulb hanging from the ceiling, a toilet behind a curtain, a hotplate with two burners, and a wobbly kitchen table with a couple of broken-down kitchen chairs. The night of the attack, Pee-wee and I both saw the steam rising from the pot on the hotplate, and my mother staring at it for an inordinate amount of time. It was clear that Mama was waiting for the water to boil because she wouldn't take her eyes off it, and we couldn't take our eyes off her. Somehow, we instinctively knew that our fate was directly connected to that large pot of water.

I can still see the scene as if it were yesterday. It's always in slow motion in my nightmares. My mother picks up the pot of "hot" water with dishtowels wrapped around the handles while I frantically try to figure out which way to run and where to hide in that closet of a room. All I know is that my feet are glued to the floor.

Mama heaves the entire pot of water over my head. As I try to shield my face with my hands, I suddenly realize that <u>I am not burning</u>. I am shivering—shivering *because the water is cold* and shivering because I have survived my mother's most heinous attack against me to date.

Mama was as shocked as Pee-wee and I that the water hadn't scalded me, and she actually seemed disappointed. I'm sure there was a perfectly logical explanation for why the water was cold, but in my little kid's mind someone had magically turned the water cold and saved me, and although I was convinced that Pee-wee and I weren't long for this world—alone in that apartment with a crazy woman—at least this once, an invisible hero had showed up and saved me.

The sun went down, came up, and went down again, and Pee-wee and I remained paralyzed on the bed. We were too frightened to ask for food, too frightened to speak, and too frightened to move. If there had not been a knock at the door on the night I later dubbed "The Invasion," I think we would have died in that darkened corner out of complete fear.

"Mrs. Maxwell," shouted the male voice behind the door, "it's Artie Rothenberg and I just need to get in for a minute to check the furnace. It will only take a minute."

"GO AWAY—WE'RE IN BED!"

"Mrs. Maxwell, I must come in for just a second. Throw on a robe or something because I'm going to use my pass-key to open the door."

At the word pass-key, Mama grabbed the butcher knife and raced toward the stairs, but as she did, the door swung open and instead of the landlord coming down the stairs, an army descended. The army consisted of four white policemen with guns drawn, two men in white coats, and Miss Sally Perkins, the social worker, hiding behind them all. As Mama chopped at the air with her butcher knife, one of the men in the white coats stabbed her with a hypodermic needle, and as the policemen held her still, they put her into a straitjacket. The sedative began to quickly take effect, and the medics laced Mama's arms across her stomach while they tied the various levels of straps behind her back. When my mother had completely lost consciousness, the men in the white coats laid her on a stretcher, put her in the back of an ambulance, and took her away.

Miss Perkins and one of the policemen drove us to a Night Court to officially be labeled "Wards of the State" so that Cuyahoga County could dispense with us as they saw fit. I broke down and cried as I've never cried before or since—big cacophonous wails. All my bravado disappeared. In that moment, instead of being the protector I became the baby and Pee-wee became the leader. She never shed a tear—not one— and the resolute steeliness that would become her life-long trademark was born that night. Although she was only five, Pee-wee grabbed my hand and patted it as if she were a sixty-year-old grandmother, and she said the words that would sustain me long after we would be separated and lose track of each other: "It's okay, Elno; we gonna' be all right." Pee-wee had spoken.

❈❈

I am discovering that there can be much tragedy and heartache in life. But to me there is a difference between the two. Tragedies tend to slam against us from some outside corporate force like 9-11, the Holocaust, WW I and II, or school shootings. Heartaches, on the other hand, always seem to be extremely personal and tend to involve rejection, betrayal, or abandonment.

Sometimes *tragedies* travel at such a pace that you can hardly catch your breath before the next one follows on the heels of the first, and they all seem bent on flattening your life into road kill. On the other hand, *heartaches* tend to pack enough power to rip your heart out and serve it back to you as pâté on day-old bread. Such was the case of the heartache brought on by the abandonment and rejection of my father. I would eventually heal, but it would take me a few decades, many prayers, many episodes of Oprah, and a lot of Maya Angelou poetry to get over the indifference of a sperm-spewer.

6
Seriously God—Wtf?

~

"Not belonging is a terrible feeling. It feels awkward and it hurts, as if you were wearing someone else's shoes."—**The Romeo And Juliet Code,** by Phoebe Stone

Do you know what I've discovered about jumping out of a frying pan? It is nearly impossible not to end up in the fire.

※※

After the King of Night Court dubbed Pee-wee and me Wards of the State, we were taken to a temporary orphanage that the judge called "The Receiving Home." On the way to the orphanage I heard Miss Perkins tell the policeman who accompanied us that even though it was past midnight, the matrons would have to open the kitchen because not to feed Pee-wee and me as soon as

possible seemed like cruel and unusual punishment. I
remember wearily climbing a long flight of stone steps
up to a brick building with large windows. At the door,
Pee-wee and I were met by a woman who was called the
Night Matron. After a brief whispered conversation between Miss Perkins and the Colored matron, we were
led into the kitchen. Pee-wee and I were so frightened
and overwhelmed that we refused to let go of each other's hand, so they picked us both up and set us down at
a table without untangling our fingers. My baby sister
and I hadn't eaten anything in days and nothing of any
substance in months. Our clothes reeked of urine and
excrement, and our bloated stomachs made us resem-
ble children fresh off the boat from the remotest part
of Africa. At least that is what the Night Matron loudly
whispered to the policeman.

For the first time, I saw Pee-wee and me through
the eyes of others. The image of neglect that we presented was reflected in the expressions on the matrons'
faces and in their Greek chorus: *"Lord, have mercy; in
all my life, I ain't never seen no babies this bad off befo'."* As
we watched the adults watching us, I searched their
faces to gain some hint about where we were, but the
only thing that looked back at us was sadness peeking
from behind the blinds of institutionalized functional-
ity as they barked instructions at each other.

*"We'll have to separate them eventually—might as
well do it sooner than later. The one in diapers will*

have to go to the nursery and sleep in a crib, even though she should be in the kindergarten dorm."
"The nine year old needs to sleep in the teen ward in a bunk bed."
"They both needs to be checked for lice and deloused befo' they heads get near any beddin'."
"First things first. Feed these babies before they faints dead away from hunger."
"Who been raisin' these chilrin'—a pack of rats?"

Even though the adult consensus was that Pee-wee and I were absolutely filthy, a humane decision was quickly made that food was needed before a bath and delousing. The Night Matron had one of her helpers open up the cafeteria kitchen and heat up the leftovers from that night's dinner. She gave Pee-wee and me a bowl of navy bean soup with globs of fat-back floating on the top, a cup of rice pudding with lumps the size of my toes, and two stale ginger snap cookies with a glass of buttermilk. Pee-wee was too frightened to eat much of the food, but I gobbled up the meal as if it were my Last Supper.

I can't ever remember anything before or after the first meal in The Receiving Home tasting as great as that bean soup/ginger snap cookie combo. *Exactly at that black-hole moment, food became my drug of choice, and I would struggle with this addiction for the rest of my life.* After two servings of everything, I licked the soup bowl twice; and then I spoke for the first time since the attempted scalding by my mother and the invasion by the police: *"People, I gotta tell ya—you done outdid your-selves! This here is the best damn food I've ever eaten!"*

❊❊

The Cuyahoga County Receiving Home for Children turned out to be a County holding tank for black children who could not get adopted or whose parents could no longer care for them.   The Receiving Home that was in one wing of a public school was extremely overcrowded when Pee-wee and I arrived. The orphanage might have been started with the best of intentions, but once children checked in, they rarely checked out.

My sister and I hardly saw each other except when I was forced to clean up Pee-wee's throw-up when her delicate stomach couldn't keep down the greasy food we were served. No one visited us, no one told us where Mama was, no matron ever spoke kindly to us or hugged us, and as long as we made our beds with perfect hospital corners every morning (something I still do until this day), we wouldn't be beaten. We stayed in The Receiving Home through both our birthdays and beyond one Christmas holiday which was marked by an orphan grab-and-go warehouse free-for-all.

Sometime before Christmas Day, all the inmates were loaded into buses and taken to a warehouse that had endless rows of used and broken toys and a seedy white Santa who looked like he was coming off a three-day bender. The idea was to have scores of poor Colored orphans sit on Santa's raggedy-ass lap (sometimes three or four at a time to make the process more efficient), and tell him what they wanted.

An indifferent caseworker with an elf's hat steered the kids to tables bearing other children's discarded toys. Pee-wee asked for a sewing machine and got a plastic toy one that was too broken to work. I asked for a purse and got one that had a broken clasp. I grabbed my sorry-ass purse and promptly ran away.

I had a mission to accomplish. Earlier on the bus ride to the Santa warehouse, an older kid had pointed out to me that one of the imposing buildings we'd passed was the main Post Office. She told me: *"If yo' daddy is as smart as you keep braggin' he is then he must work at the Post Office. That's where all the smart Colored men's work, stackin' mail in the basement or deliverin' letters and shit to the Colored neighborhoods, and they gots stripes down the sides of their pants just like you keep talkin' about. You should go to the Post Office and see if they has your daddy."*

This seemed as if it might be a second chance to find the man who was supposed to be my father. I don't know what I thought I'd do with him if I saw him again—maybe I thought I could convince him to like me and come and rescue Pee-wee and me. Hope always springs eternal in children where parents are concerned, and logic is not the strong suit of the heart. I just knew that what I really wanted for Christmas was to get Pee-wee and me out of The Receiving Home, and that nasty-ass warehouse Santa sure couldn't make that dream come true.   So I slipped out of the building when no one was looking and went in search of my father.

When I entered the main Post Office, I crossed a hallway and climbed the most imposing steps in the largest stone building I'd ever seen in my life.   I marched up to the top of the stone steps where a white man stood behind an elevated podium surveying the foot traffic below him that was doing business with the clerks on the other side of the room.   I stood on my tip-toes and shouted up to the man with striped pants and asked the one question I most needed to know as a nine-year-old girl who still thought she deserved a father: "Have you seen my daddy? His name is Mr. Maxwell and he works with the letters."

After asking what my father's first name was and getting nothing but a wide-eyed, confused stare from me, the white man in the tower looked down at me for the longest time as if I were an alien and finally announced to me and everyone within shouting distance what I already suspected: *Little girl, there are a lot of men who work here but none who would willingly claim you as his kid.*

As I slowly made my way out of the building and back to the flea-market Christmas party for orphans, I had an epiphany: Pee-wee and I might stay at The Receiving Home forever because I could think of absolutely no one who was interested in finding us or cared if we lived or died.

✳✳

A couple of months later, after my unnoticed excursion to the Post Office, I woke up screaming one night from pain so debilitating that it seemed someone was ripping out my insides with an ice pick. As I nauseously sat up on the top of the bunk bed doubled over in pain, I saw a blazing fire outside the large windows behind me. In my pain-ridden delirium I thought I was in my recurring nightmare of being in the claws of The Boogey and was being dragged down into Hell.

As I began to recognize my surroundings, I noticed that my pajamas were soaking wet so I climbed down the ladder to go to the bathroom. When I got into the light, I almost forgot the pain as I stared incomprehensibly at my pajama bottoms which were completely soaked in blood. And then the reason for this dawned on me.

"THE BOOGEY AND THE CHEESE MAN ARE HERE! THE CHEESE MAN HAS FOUND ME, THE CHEESE MAN AND THE BOOGEY ARE GONNA KILL ME AND PEE-WEE," I screamed my Paul Revere cry as I ran as fast as I could to the matrons' station down the hall.

"The Boogey started a fire outside my window and he's gonna drag Pee-wee and me into Hell and burn us up. I gotta tell Pee-wee so that we can hide," I said to the matrons as I fled back down the hall toward my sister's dorm. The night matrons were playing cards and barely stopped the rhythm of their nightly ritual as they doubled over in laughter at my hysteria.

Finally, one of the matrons stopped me before I reached Pee-wee's dorm, gave me new underwear and PJ's, and slammed a hot water bottle into my hands as she forcefully pushed me back into bed. The matron then shot me a parting tagline as she chuckled to herself all of the way back to the card table: "That's not Hell-fire you see out that window, chil'; it's the refinery across the way. Although it probably seems like Hell to the people who work there, I suspect."

That was it. No explanation or necessary supplies ever accompanied the hot water bottle that I was given to ease the pain on several occasions after that. I officially entered womanhood at the age of nine years old between a 6 No Trump that got usurped by a 7 Uptown challenge in Bid Whist. After the great bloody debut, I never bothered to alert anyone again about its recurrence every month; I just crawled into a fetal position from the mind-numbing pain and cried and prayed that God would not let The Boogey/Cheese Man find me. I was now convinced that The Boogey and The Cheese Man had morphed into one giant monster. I surreptitiously hid the bloody underwear and clothes in the bottom of my trunk at the foot of the bed so it couldn't follow the smell of my blood and take me out. I was cognizant of the fact that I needed more information if I was going to be able to survive this new monster manifestation that could give a command from far away and cause blood to leak from my body. It was clear that the matrons of The Receiving Home didn't have a clue as to the blood-letting caused by monsters.

❈❈

By the time an "Aunt Lily" showed up (claiming to be my mother's older sister), Pee-wee and I had probably been in The Receiving home for about nine months. Aunt Lily was barely five feet tall and didn't weigh over ninety pounds when she was soaking wet. She wore her hair in a tight sideways bun and sported little round spectacles perched on the permanently judgmental grimace on her face. When this woman who I had never seen before in my life came to rescue us from the orphanage, she was dressed in a worn but stiffly starched and pressed shirt-waist dress, and a dark brown coat with a matching hat. I almost called her Mama because she was the spitting image of my mother except one could almost hear the chorus singing "Onward Christian Soldiers" behind her.

Aunt Lily inherited a sickly, mostly mute six year old still in diapers and a street-wise ten-year-old with three months' worth of blood-stained underwear. When Aunt Lily transferred my clothes into the suitcase she had brought and came across the offending garments, she recoiled from me as if I were carrying the Bubonic Plague.

"Where did this blood come from, child?" demanded Aunt Lily.

"The Cheese Man or The Boogey Man—I don't know which one done it. They both was messin' wit me, and they came after me from Queen Maxine's house," I replied.

❊❊

I stood outside the door of the Matron's office to eavesdrop when my "claim of being defiled" as Aunt Lily phrased it, was being investigated by The Receiving Home at Aunt Lily's urgings. "I'm not taking this child home with me until you tell me why she bleeds at ten years old and has all these crazy stories about a Cheese Man. The Devil is afoot here, and I'm going to get to the bottom of it," said Aunt Lily.

The Receiving Home got Queen Maxine on the phone, and she and Aunt Lily talked to each other for a very, very long time. I could overhear my Aunt's "tsks" and expressions of "oh Sweet Jesus" and "what burden has the Lord given me now" as she punctuated her responses with moans and groans. After the phone call was over, my Sunday-go-to-meeting-hat-and-gloved-church-lady aunt didn't utter another word until we were all established in her sanctimonious come-to-Jesus home. She came out of the Matron's office, finished packing my suitcase, took Pee-wee by the hand, and with the look of a person that has just encountered Satan's offspring, motioned me to follow her out the door. As I obediently trailed behind my newfound aunt, I contemplated the benediction I had overheard in her summation of me to the Matron.

"I don't care much for the sinful harlot who calls herself Maxine," chirped Aunt Lily, "but I believe her when she says my sister let Eleanor run wild. I know my younger sister and she is as crazy as a loon. I signed the papers today to have her officially committed to the county mental institution for the rest of her life, and now I need to raise her children, though the Lord only knows where I'm going to get the strength to handle that little hellion of hers. According to Eleanor's caseworker, her school records verify that she is a little demon—completely and totally out of control. This is what I know for sure: whatever happened in that harlot's house, my niece brought it on herself."

❄❄❄

"They call it 'The Curse,'" said the petite, prim, be-spectacled Aunt Lily from her kitchen stool. Although Aunt Lily's vocabulary was mostly "Bible-speak," what she spoke was in perfect, articulate, clipped English and, like my mother, it was an extreme source of pride to her that she didn't "speak like the other Colored folks" in her neighborhood.

"It was given to women by God because we are such sinful creatures," pontificated my holier-than-thou Aunt Lily. "It comes once a month to remind us that we've been cursed, and when it arrives you need to pin these folded rags to your underwear so that the blood won't soak through your drawers. I'll show you how to wash and scrub them clean in the wash tub over there. If you scrub them hard enough you'll be able to get all the stains out. The most important thing you must know about 'The Curse' is, if you even kiss a boy—Lord have mercy—if you even hold a boy's hand, you'll get a baby in your belly just as fast as you can sneeze. That would make you a little whore—just like your older sister, Bernice."

I had just met my Half-Sister-Aunt Bernice for the first time. She'd briefly come down from Detroit to have a screaming match with my Aunt Lily about permanently locking Mama away in a mental institution. It was then that she wasted no time bursting my bubble about my noble birth and being named after "some famous white man's old lady."

While I was trying to imagine what a "whore" was and if that had anything to do with Foxy Clarisse's line of work, suddenly a light bulb went off in my head. I knew that this Aunt Lily was going to be a treasure trove of information. She had already informed me about a monster curse and that girls could get a baby in their stomachs by just touching a boy. *My fortunes were looking up!* This woman was not my Aunt—this woman was a Colored Glinda, the Good Witch of the East! I'd seen the movie, and I knew that I'd finally hit the mother lode by finding my dear Aunt Lily.

"Hot damn, woman, you are amazing," I said as I excitedly positioned myself on my chair to properly engage in conversation with this woman who seemed to be so savvy about monster effects. Here was an adult who was finally willing to help me understand what was going on. Seated on a chair directly in front of Aunt Lily, I excitedly crossed my chubby legs, cupped one cheek in my right hand while gesticulating with the other hand, and cozily leaned in towards my new confidant. I'd been trying to find someone like her all my life—someone who could help me with all of my questions. Finally, I was going to get some answers!

"Jesus H. Christ!" I said. "Who would have thought; there's another monster called, The Curse?"

For a brief moment, Aunt Lily froze in place with her mouth agape, and then all hell broke loose.

"DEMON-SEED. . .shut your filthy mouth! DON'T YOU EVER use the Lord's name in vain in my house or disrespect me like that again! This is the Lord's house—THE LORD'S HOUSE—and I am 'Aunt Lily' to you, you little sassy bold-faced demon, and Jesus is your God, not a curse word. I will not put up with your shenanigans, DO YOU HEAR ME?

You're just like your whorish mother—full of evil and sass—and just like your mother you're going to Hell in a hand basket on the next train out of here!"

On that final note of searing judgment, my good witch—my rescuer—cupped her hand into a clawed weapon and slammed it into the side of my mouth with the force of a threatened cassowary bird. I saw stars, spit up blood, and promptly fell off the chair at her feet. As I looked up at her through my blurred vision, her fiery eyes seemed to flash lightning bolts over the wire-rimmed spectacles on the tip of her nose. When she raised her deadly hand again with the warning that she was going to knock me into all of next week—separating parts of my body into each day—the only thing I could think of was one of The Queen's favorite expressions: *What the fuck—out of the frying pan into the fire!"* But I did not say what I was thinking—for the time being, Aunt Lily had won.

※※

I am discovering that the most significant things about abandonment are the inability to be heard and the feeling of not belonging. The story has it that even Jesus was abandoned by God on the cross and when he cried out: "My God, my God, why have you forsaken me," poor JC got no response—"bupkis." *What was up with that?* The inability to belong and thus be heard must be at the core of every suicide because nothing—absolutely nothing—could be more devastating in the dark night of the soul than that. So why is it that some people get up again, bounce back, rise from the dead, and keep trying to find the path home—to belonging—to having their story heard—while many others languish at sea?

7

The Church Lady

~

"God gave us our relatives; thank God we can choose our friends."—**Ethel Watts Mumford**

Do you know what I've discovered about Moses and the Ten Commandments? I can't prove it, but I think another person was there on Mount Sinai when God gave Moses his two tablets bearing the ten rules that Jews were supposed to live by in the midst of their pagan neighbors. I'm pretty sure my Aunt Lily was hiding behind one of the rocks and eavesdropped on the chat between God and Moses. How else could she have carved out her own set of "Thirteen Commandments All Negroes Should Live By in the Midst of Heathens?" I'm just sayin'—when I arrived at Aunt Lily's house in the 1950s—these thirteen commandments were in full force and were treated like they had been passed down from the mouth of God Himself.

✳✲✳

Aunt Lily was the oldest of fourteen children. Her Cherokee mother and preacher man father were long dead by the time Pee-wee and I showed up, and many of their children were scattered to parts unknown—most engulfed by alcoholism or mental illness. My aunt left home to marry a WWII soldier and settled in Cleveland after the war. Two sisters followed her: my mother and Aunt Celine—also a paranoid-schizophrenic wall chatterer. Aunt Lily reared all her sisters' offspring. The cruel irony of Aunt Lily's altruism is that she only had one child, and he was born with Down syndrome. Since no one knew what that was in the black community at the time, he was simply labeled retarded, and my uncle resented his handicap all of my cousin's life. In a rare moment of vulnerability one day, I overheard Aunt Lily say that because of the sins of her father, all of his offspring bore the mark of Cain, and her most of all.

My mother's sister was the antithesis of Queen Maxine. Aunt Lily was poor but her philosophy was: *"We may be poor, but we don't have to be filthy, disorderly, uncouth, immoral, or heathens."* Even though the railroad tracks were directly behind her Cleveland doubles house, and the train unhinged every picture and mirror several times a day when it passed by, she systematically went back and course-corrected the pictures every time and within minutes of the train's passing.

Cleanliness was truly next to godliness as far as Aunt Lily was concerned, and other than using the Lord's name in vain, being dirty was just about the worst sin a person could commit. My aunt constantly scrubbed and cleaned, patched and mended, combed and straightened every inch of her house and us. Magnificent crocheted doilies covered every chair and beautiful cascading curtains covered every window, while intricate handmade quilts covered every bed. A germaphobe could eat off her floors without hesitancy, and a doctor could perform an emergency operation in her sink and bathtub without ever having to sterilize them. And Aunt Lily had retained and cultivated much of the Cherokee medicinal remedies for life's ills. She was into holistic medicine before it ever became popular.

The first thing she did when she took Pee-wee and me out of The Receiving Home was diagnose our physical and spiritual health within ten minutes.

"Pee-wee: Worms, asthma, psoriasis, migraine headaches, and the saddest baby I've ever seen—don't you ever smile, child?"

"Eleanor: Worms, demons, more demons, and sassiest child I've ever seen—don't you ever stop chattering, Demon-seed?"

After anointing me with oil to "purge the demons" from my body, she attacked the worms in both of us by shoving down our throats a three-times-a-day concoction of cod liver oil, lemon juice, crushed raw pumpkin seeds, crushed cloves, wormwood extract, and hot peppers. Everything but the kitchen sink was flushed from our intestines within 24 hours. Some of the intestinal inhabitants were still wiggling when they hit the commode, as Aunt Lily liked to call the toilet. Since she grew her own vegetables, made her own bread and preserves, canned her own fruits and vegetables, and made her own medicinal salves, it didn't take long for us to begin to thrive physically, if not emotionally. I resented the loss of freedom that it cost to be immaculate and saved, and I expressed my rebellion whenever I got a chance.

※❉※

Even though Aunt Lily was a member of one of the oldest and largest black churches in Cleveland, she had her own personal version of holiness and it was more in keeping with rabbinic law than Christianity. I think she felt that the more legalistic a woman could become, the more distance she could put between herself and sin, and the better her chances of "getting over" in a world she couldn't control. Aunt Lily even had her own personal "thirteen" commandments because she had found at least that many that she was convinced God had missed:

1. Thou shall not wear red ("only whores wear red").
2. Thou shall not wear makeup ("only sluts, Cubans, Italians, and your half-sister Bernice wear makeup").

3. Thou must cover your head at all times when entering the temple of the Holy God ("the Jews have missed it on a lot of things, but on this rule, they have got it right").

4. Thou must always wear a dress on Sunday and only wear pants during the week if you're a child ("pants, low cut dresses, and exposed knees are the Devil's temptation and lead a woman to whoredom").

5. Thou must always wear clean underwear ("you never know when you'll get hit by a bus and your dress is thrown up over your head; no need to give the Devil an entryway").

6. Thou shall honor the Sabbath ("turning on a light or stove on the Sabbath is violating God's Law and He'll strike you dead, for sure").

7. Thou shall not play cards, drink or gamble, go dancing, laugh, crack a smile, run and play on the Sabbath, or in any way give an indication that you could be happy ("those things are the Devil's merriment").

8. Thou shall not listen to any music other than church music ("that Colored bumpin' and grindin' music is straight from the Devil's pipe organ in Hell").

9. Thou shall not daydream ("idle hands are the Devil's workshop").

10. Thou shall not covet thy neighbors' money or toys ("lusting for money and toys is the root of all evil").

11. Thou shall not be slovenly ("white people and Jews are always watching us").

12. Thou shall fast and pray from sundown on Saturday until midday on Sundays and never miss Wednesday night prayer meetings ("so help you God, or He will strike you dead").

13. Thou must repent of thy many sins every Saturday like clockwork ("every Saturday will be our Negro version of Yom Kippur and every Sunday dinner will be our Negro Seder where we give thanks to the Lord for all his glorious bounty because the Jews sure got it right"). Amen? Amen!

※❊※

As soon as I saw which way the wind blew with Aunt Lily, I immediately "got saved." I marched home one day from Vacation Bible School with a Bible clutched to my ten-year-old chest in my right hand, and my left hand lifted in a perfect jazz-hand wave, while my body did a Holy Ghost jig, and my head tilted up to the heavens in praise. "Halle-LU-jah-it's-a-miracle,-thank-you-Jesus,-I've-been-saved, sanctified-and-glorified—PRAISE YOUR HOLY NAME–*JEE-ZUS!*"

For thirty minutes my life with Aunt Lily was sheer bliss. She cried and hugged me for the first and last time in my life. She fed me her prize church-lady dessert: homemade gingerbread cake with lemon sauce. Aunt Lily called me Eleanor instead of Demon-seed. For thirty heavenly minutes I was loved, I was cherished, I was adored, and then I stubbed my toe. . . .

"Shit, goddamnit, mother-fuckin', ASSHOLE ICE BOX!!"

Sanctified-and-saved Aunt Lily furiously dragged me down the hall by the straps on my overalls to wash my mouth out with lye soap. While she boxed my ears at rapid-fire speed, all I could hear through the ringing in my head was a familiar verbal baptism: *"You're going straight to Hell, DEMON-SEED—straight to Hell, do you hear me? This time you've crossed over the line."*

❈❈

"IT'S YO' MOUF," screamed an impatient Pee-wee through four missing top teeth as she threw her hands in the air in total exasperation. She was eight years old, and she was standing over my semi-conscious body that had been knocked down a long flight of wooden steps by Aunt Lily.

I had overheard the neighbors talking about a young Colored man who had come to Cleveland in 1956. He had come north to preach about Negro rights and how our time was long overdue. So when Aunt Lily gave me the chore of scrubbing down the stairs on my hands and knees when I wanted to go out and play, I got angry and promptly told her that she wouldn't always have me to be her personal slave, "because times were a-changing for Colored folks, and I plan to demand my God-given rights around here." Unfortunately, I delivered this speech at the top of the stairs, allowing for a long and painful tumble when she backhanded me across the face for my "demon-possessed, sassy mouth." Timing has never been my strong suit.

"You jesth don't know when to shuth up, do you?" As Pee-wee scolded me, standing over me with both fists perched on her tiny hips, I couldn't help but notice how much she had become a pint-sized per-sonification of Aunt Lily. With a stern look she con-tinued to sanctimoniously lecture me as I tried to see if I would ever be able to walk again. "I'm tellin' you Chub-chub [a new nickname that Pee-wee had bap-tized me with owing to my ever-expanding body and its love affair with food]; you bring deeze problems on youself. Jesth, shuth up! SHUTH UP! I don't like all disss scrubbin' and cleanin' either, but at leasss we have food and dere are no monsters here."

Poor, naïve Pee-wee.

※※

Pee-wee bought into Aunt Lily's bullshit because my Aunt cured her migraine headaches, eradicated Pee-wee's skin problems, and taught her to sew like a min-iature master tailor. Aunt Lily fell in love with Pee-wee and to this day my sister considers Aunt Lily the only mother she ever had. Something about me irked Aunt Lily and something about my aunt royally pissed me off. I now know that no matter how perfect I tried to be, she would never have been able to get past the part of me that irritated her so much—I was the spitting image of my mother.

We lived with Aunt Lily, Uncle Oscar, and Cousin Richard for three years. Even as an adult my cousin had that sweetness that is unmistakable in most Down syndrome children, but he stayed in the background and out of the way because he was terrified of his father. Everyone was afraid of Uncle Oscar because he was that kind of evil that only ignorance and meanness can beget. Most of all, he bore the eyes of the Cheese Man, and I recognized that truth the first time I encountered him. For three years Uncle Oscar stalked me in Aunt Lily's tiny upstairs apartment. When I'd be asleep, I could sense his presence while he smoked a cigar and stared at me—leaning against the doorpost of my bedroom at the top of the stairs—willing me to him. If I was assigned to weed the garden, within ten minutes of starting my chore, I could feel his eyes on my ass. For the most part I managed to side-step him, but one night right after my twelfth birthday I was left home alone to clean up the kitchen while Aunt Lily and Pee-wee went to Wednesday night prayer. Cousin Richard was at his job as a janitor and I thought Uncle Oscar was out playing poker as he usually did on Wednesday nights. I didn't know he was there until the smell of cigar smoke and whiskey that was Uncle Oscar's tell, permeated my nostrils as I felt his hot breath against the back of my neck. Without thinking, I channeled the spirit of my mother. I grabbed the butcher knife from the dish drain and turned around. Blinded by my rage, I accidentally tripped over a kitchen chair and fell on my face. The fall probably saved my uncle's life, but I scared the shit out of his black ass as I tried to stab him to death. In his effort to escape, he fell down the flight of stairs that Aunt Lily had previously knocked me down, but he managed to hobble to his car and drive himself to the church. Pee-wee said he came in the door screaming and hollering that I had gone crazy like my mother and had tried to kill him in his own house.

"Either that heifer goes, or I go, and I means what I says," screamed Uncle Oscar to Aunt Lily and the rest of the Bible study group. "You got twenty-four hours, woman, to send that hellion back to the hole you dug her out of or you better start looking for a new husband."

❋❋

The next day, I met the third social worker assigned to our case. Because they all looked like the first Miss Perkins (young, naïve, blonde, and clueless) Pee-wee and I never learned their names—we called them all Miss Perkins. So as Pee-wee and I stood looking forlornly at each other, "Miss Perkins (#3)" and Aunt Lily loaded my stuff into the trunk of the social worker's car. Miss Perkins III recited the game plan of my fate to Aunt Lily and assured her that after a return to The Receiving Home, she would try and find a foster home that could handle me, although she couldn't promise much. This new caseworker that I'd never met and who never bothered to ask me why I tried to kill my uncle, cold-bloodedly announced her assessment of my character to everyone within earshot of the curb: "Obviously, if Eleanor feels it is necessary to attack her own uncle who has so graciously given her a home, just because he asked her to do a simple household chore, then she is probably only fit to go to the detention home for wayward youths."

Upon hearing this verdict on my life, my heart was so full of fear that it almost burst. I turned to plead with Aunt Lily to let me explain. She scorned me and refused to look at me, but when I walked past her to get into the social worker's car, I heard Aunt Lily whisper a barely audible absolution: *"I believe you; God have mercy on me, but I do believe you, child."*

Pee-wee told me from that point on Aunt Lily never let my sister out of her sight, and within months of my departure my aunt sent Pee-wee to a foster home to help her escape Uncle Oscar. Aunt Lily would continue to co-exist with her monster of a husband and cling to her religion until the day she died.

For years I hated Aunt Lily for not protecting me from my uncle. I hated her for splitting up Pee-wee and me because it would be more than a year before we saw each other again. And other than a brief season in the same foster home when we were in our teens, my sister and I would never live together again as children.

Pee-wee told me years later that as she sat by Aunt Lily's death bed, my aunt made the belated confession: *"Tell Eleanor I'm sorry, and I always loved her."*

I am discovering that life is a bitch. It can be one endless monster attack after the other, and it can take years to undo the aftermath. When I was thirty-seven years old, I had almost erased Aunt Lily from my heart and memory. I had lived abroad as an expatriate and was flying back to the United States. Someone had casually given me a book to read on the plane to help me pass the time. It did more than that; it drop-kicked me right back to my aunt and uncle's house beside the railroad tracks on Norman Avenue.

I did not cry when Pee-wee and I were ripped apart at Aunt Lily's house that horrific day, but I did cry for seven non-stop hours while crossing the Atlantic as I read **The Color Purple** by Alice Walker. When I got to the part where "Mr." forces Nettie to leave her sister, Celie, I turned my face to the window and I wept uncontrollably until there were no more tears left for the years the cankerworm had stolen from my little sister and me. I wept for Aunt Lily who, like Celie, had had no other option in life but to stay in a loveless marriage with a monster in order for her and her Down syndrome child to survive. I forgave my aunt at that moment and asked her to forgive me for not fully understanding the ways of monsters and the suffering they caused in the lives of impoverished black women in the 1960s.

8

Angelou, Twain, and T.H. White—Oh My!

~

"Never before had I felt trapped, seduced, and caught up in story. . . I had never known the pleasure of reading, of exploring the recesses of the soul, of letting myself be carried away by imagination, beauty, and the mystery of fiction and language."— **The Shadow of the Wind,** by Carlos Ruiz Zafón

Do you know what I discovered while dwelling amongst the Lotus Eaters? I found the ability to be turned inside out, upside down, and flung deliriously high into the sky by: *books!*

✺❂✺

If I made my life into a movie, the ages of twelve through sixteen would open with the scene of a revolving door sporting a neon sign over it flashing the words, "Abusive Foster Homes 6, 7, 8 and Counting." The film would show me entering and exiting, always clutching the same suitcase, never able to actually find a place to call home, and in a state of permanent emotional whiplash.

I really tried to get along with my various families. I tried to make each foster home work, but on any given day I'd come home from school and see the car of my case-worker-of-the-month out front and then notice my suitcase on the front porch (my foster parents' way of demonstrating who was really in control). I was not a bad kid by today's standards or even the standards of that time. I was just a mouthy kid with an outspoken sense of justice, without a filter.

"You know there are child-labor laws against these types of things you keep making me do, don't you? If I wanted to, I could really get your ass in trouble." (My sorry-ass suitcase and I get kicked to the curb to wait for Miss Perkins #26 to take me to another foster home.)

"Does my caseworker know that the money Welfare sends you to buy me clothes is being spent on your 'real kid' while I have to wear these nasty-ass clothes from Goodwill? They smell like dog shit!" (My face is slapped and my ass is beat with a two-by-four, and then my sorry-ass suitcase and I are shown the door to wait on the front stoop for Miss Perkins #28.)

*"Oooooh-weee, does your husband know you been tippin'
out on him while he works the night shift—does he REALLY
know what's going on in this house?"* (I am met at the
school by Miss Perkins #30 with my sorry-ass suitcase
in hand because there is no marriage or home to
return to anymore.)

Constant logorrhea leaked low-ball questions out
of my mouth in a steady stream of rushing words *before*
I fell in love. After I fell in love, my questions took on
the weaponry of the *Grand Inquisitor.*

❊❊

The year I turned fourteen a newly graduated, wet-
behind-the-ears-ennui-clad white teacher took it upon
herself to teach ghetto children the Dewey Decimal
System. I honestly think she forgot her lesson plans
that day and pulled the assignment out of her butt.
It was obvious by her lackadaisical attitude that she
wished she were anywhere but there—teaching black
kids to whom she once announced, "you are incapable
of learning anything." After thoroughly grilling us on
what seemed like a numbering maze from Hell, the
teacher asked the class how many students had been
to the main public library downtown and how many of
us had library cards.

Except for those who were asleep, the rest of the
class stared at the teacher—thinking she had lost her
ever-lovin' mind. Our school certainly didn't have a

library and none of us had ever been in a library or even knew anybody who had been in a library. So she gave us an assignment to go to the Cleveland Public Library near Public Square, get a library card, locate a book we wanted to read using the Dewey Decimal system, and turn in a two-paragraph report—one paragraph on our library experience and one paragraph on the book we had chosen.

I have no idea why I decided to do the assignment. I could read, but I don't remember how I learned. I certainly had never read a book from cover to cover before, nor had I read one for pleasure. I had perfect attendance because I'd always come to school to get rest from being used as a child laborer until all hours of the night. That meant I had slept through most of my classes. I don't remember ever reviewing any textbooks, taking exams, or doing any homework. I must have—I just don't remember it, and it couldn't have been of any great quality. My guess is that I got passed from grade to grade with the lowest grades possible. It really is a conundrum to me that I can remember so many vivid things from the age of four but not one official report card or school experience until I entered ninth grade.

I'd do almost anything to get out of my foster home for a Saturday afternoon, and I think taking my teacher's library challenge appealed to my sense of adventure. It gave me a chance to explore the inside of a building in the Public Square area which was the domain of the white world—nobody I knew ever went there.   I knew that the library was somewhere near the main post office, and who knew—there was always a chance I might run into my father.

It took me awhile to find the main library but when I did, I walked into a sea of architectural wonders— the main library not being the least of them.   I had never seen anything so beautiful in my entire life.   The library had what I would later learn were Corinthian columns, vaulted stenciled ceilings, exquisite chandeliers, beautiful marble floors, and the head of a helmeted woman (Athena—the goddess of wisdom and patron of war) standing guard over the entryway.

How could I have been born in Cleveland and not have known this place existed?   *And the light!*   Up until then, I never realized that windows were meant to give unobstructed access to the sunlight.   As fastidious as Aunt Lily was about personal cleanliness, she never won the battle over the dust-encrusted windows caused by all the coal trains passing within an arm's length of her house.

The light streamed like beams from heaven through double-storied arched windows, and here the dust particles danced in the avenues of light in a resounding chorus that seemingly sang: *"Welcome, Eleanor—we've been waiting for you!"*   Then another sensory perception co-mingled with that vision—the smell of old books.   I am now in my sixties and I have never smelled a perfume, a gourmet meal, or a flower garden that makes me as weak in the knees as that of an old collection of books.

A kind, old, white lady, who seemed amused at my wonderment, sat behind a desk that was labeled, "Librarian." She helped me navigate the card system and taught me what the different multi-layered sections of the library meant. The Librarian went out of her way to explain how most books could be borrowed while some were just to be referenced for special projects and couldn't leave their library home. I had no idea that I stood in a place that would one day become the third largest research library in the country; I just knew that I had died and gone to heaven and nothing bad could happen in a place like that.

I spent an hour just savoring the cards in the wooden trays that stretched throughout the first floor. I began to experiment with the Dewey Decimal System by tracing books I found in the catalogues to their shelf locations and discovered it was like solving a hide-and-seek game—but with books. After watching me wander around for some time, the librarian asked me what kind of stories I liked, and I answered with the first thing that popped into my mind: "I like shit that's funny."

The librarian introduced me to Mr. Twain.

I plopped down on the library floor in the middle of the stacks and began to read **The Adventures of Tom Sawyer**! It was an orgasmic experience because it was the first time something I read made me laugh—laugh so hard that I almost peed my pants and received my first golden "shish" from a librarian. I was transported by the life of a bad-ass white kid, and I fled my painful existence by becoming absorbed in the fictional life of an orphan boy with a temperament similar to mine.

Within two weeks, I was devouring **The Adventures of Huckleberry Finn.** I read it with a flashlight underneath my bed covers in the middle of the night in a foster home that equated reading with showing off. I don't remember how I did on the anemic book report, but from that moment on, that library and all libraries became my sanctuary and books became my salvation.

Once I had consumed several Mark Twain books I went looking for other libraries and other librarians closer to home, and they turned me on to historical fiction. When I closed the last pages of **Gone with the Wind** and **Uncle Tom's Cabin**, I fantasized for weeks how I would write the sequels and get Rhett to "give a damn" again, and knew that at least one of my foster fathers was the evil embodiment of Simon Legree.

Librarians guided me into Arthurian fantasy and British mysteries. When I finished T.H. White's **The Once and Future King** and Agatha Christie's **Murder on the Orient Express,** I came away with the firm conviction that I could never spend the rest of my life in Cleveland when there was such a rich, wide world of experiences to be had on this planet. The East Side of Cleveland was my prison but books gave me freedom and truth—truths that set me free from the tyranny of monsters and gave me hope that I could get out and stay out of Central Avenue.

A newfound friend took me to a section of the library that I thought she had made up: *Negro Literature*. She introduced me to the poetry and stories of Langston Hughes—a man the librarian said had graduated from Central High which was not too far from where I lived. His poetry and stories made my heart hurt in recognition of the suffering he described, and they made me swell with pride that he was so smart.

After leaving Langston, I stumbled into **Go Tell it on the Mountain** by James Baldwin. His book made me weep with rage and turned me into an atheist—if only for a season. Baldwin's books piqued my thirst for the genius of Richard Wright's **Native Son** which opened up my heart to start seeing the potential Bigger Thomas in me.

Once I had fallen in love with reading, I fell in love with learning, and when I fell in love with learning, I fell in love with school. At first, there were so many unfamiliar words that reading actually hurt my head, but I subsequently purchased my first dictionary and it became my constant companion until the binding disintegrated, the pages slipped away, and my mind no longer needed Webster to fill in the blanks.

On any given day I would phonetically sound out new words and memorize their meanings. If you look carefully today at a number of books in the Cleveland Public Library system, the reader will probably still discover various words that are faintly underlined in pencil that I forgot to erase, so that I could look up their definitions at a later time.

I found a refuge in books and school that became transcendental—no one could invade it, no matter how evil they were. Unfortunately (or maybe, fortunately), my love of reading empowered my unfiltered "mouf" with even more ammunition against the caretakers who abused me.

※◈※

I am discovering as I grow older that reading became the means of an exodus from a world of monsters that came out to play the day I was born. I don't go anywhere without a book because I know that if I can't handle the disappointments or time-sucks thrust upon me, I can always assuage my heart and mind through reading. There will always be somewhere else to go between the pages of another world that is far more appealing than the one I'm currently occupying—a world that gives me perspective and an opportunity to be healed. Because of my love for reading, Mark Twain fortified my humor, Agatha Christie taught me critical thinking, Langston Hughes gave me a worldview, and Maya Angelou helped heal a little girl with a story similar to hers and taught her to "know why the caged bird sings."

9

Revenge Served Cold

~

"Sure, if I reprehend anything in this world it is the use of my oracular tongue, and a nice derangement of epitaphs!"—Mrs. Malaprop from **The Rivals,** a play by Richard Sheridan

Do you know what I've discovered about words? A fool and a wise man can have equal access to the same vocabulary, but only the wise man will know when to keep his mouth shut.

❊❊

One of the cruelest and most ignorant foster mothers I ever had was a motor-mouth of a woman by the name of Rowena Burley—the "Mrs. Malaprop" of Kinsman Avenue. Burley-pig, as she was derisively known to me, had the looks of a female Idi Amin, the body of a giant walrus, and skin the color of asphalt. Her face bore a jagged scar from the right corner of her lip to the top of her right ear—souvenir of a knife attack by an intruder in a mansion in Shaker Heights where she had once worked as a domestic. She was married to a harmless little slip of a man who worked three jobs to make ends meet and whose balls got clipped on his wedding day. Although I was required to call Mr. Burley "Daddy," he never spoke a word to me other than good morning and good night. It didn't take long to figure out that Ernest Leroy Burley worked three jobs to escape his wife more than he needed to make a living, and what she did or how she ran his home was of little importance to him.

When I visited the Burley's home at the age of fourteen, I was told by my Miss Perkins (#48) that there were two other children living there who would be wonderful playmates for me.

As I entered the house for the first time, I immediately bypassed the nondescript, ten-year-old son of my new parents, but I turbo-charged the quiet little girl with Tweety-Bird eyes who was glued to the wall and threw my arms around her.

"Pee-wee!" I cried. "I didn't know YOU were gonna be the other foster kid living here!"

"Well, isn't that nice that the two of them know each other," said my clueless caseworker to Rowena Burley.

As Pee-wee and I hugged each other (me grinning from ear to ear and her just staring down at her feet), it never occurred to me to wonder why my case-worker didn't know that Pee-wee and I were sisters. I really didn't care at that time—all I knew was that we were back together again. But I could tell something was wrong with Pee-wee. She seemed really nervous and fidgety as if she were trying to tell me something. Pee-wee didn't talk at all but kept shaking her head as Burley-pig gave us the grand tour of her tiny cookie-cutter house that had been ordered as a kit from the Sears and Roebuck catalogue by the previous white owner before "white flight" had hit the neighborhood.

"Why don't y'all come into the livin' room and make yo'selves declinable." Burley-pig practically sang her next line as she impersonated what she thought a rich white woman would say as we toured her "mansion": *I gots whore-doors and drinks for allllllllll.*

As we stepped onto the carpet (covered entirely in thick plastic), the boy took a running leap to the organ bench while the rest of us tiptoed our way through a living room so full of Sears Catalogue items (lamps, end tables, and a buffet sideboard all covered in plastic), we had to walk single-file in order to get to a couch and two chairs. Our feet burped their way across the plastic on the floor, while my caseworker's high heels hole-punched their way in and out of the plastic runway to the nearest chair. When Pee-wee and I collapsed onto the couch, our butts simultaneously connected with the plastic seat cushions. Without warning, our asses became the loud speakers of giants' farts. We had entered plastic hell!

"This here's our anointed livin' room that we constrains for our most impotents of guests," said the preening Mrs. Burley as her walrus ass connected to the couch that belched the final plastic-fart welcome.

When my caseworker asked me if "this seemed like a foster home that you could be happy in," what the hell was I supposed to say? It seemed like a plastic insane asylum, but Pee-wee lived there; I had no choice but to stay. However, I'd already been in enough foster homes to know there would be an "unveiling" of the real lady of the manor, and within forty-eight hours the lilting, preening, malapropism-spewing Rowena Burley gave way to the caustic, mean-spirited, ignorant Burley-pig of a bitch whom I would come to know and despise.

✳✦✳

"**Primarilyist:** My boy is the onlyest one 'lowed in the livin' room so that he cans play with his organ. He's gonna be famous like Nat King Cole someday—a true pronouncement of our race. I betta' not catch yo' little fat ass and yo' sister's ugly bug-eyed face in my parlor messin' wit my boy's instrument," said the pig-faced Rowena as her son stared at us with the disdain of a boy-king presiding over a court of peasants.

"**Secondarily:** Elnura, let's me give you some advertisement, chil'. You way too ugly and stupid to have the friends you do. You needs to hang out wit people uglier and stupeedier than you is (if you can find 'em, hee, hee, hee), 'cause it don't help yo' case none to have smart, glamor-pussing friends—it jes pontificates yo' patheticism.

"**Thirdesly:** My boy gets the chicken thighs—y'all gets the neck bones and the chicken's butt, and you best be happy wit' it cause in most places you wouldn't even get that. It's only cause I'm a good Christian woman and considers it my God-fearin' dutability to provide a home for you wayward chilrens of the worl' that I even lets you into my manor born—so's you best be grateful for everythin' I gives you.

"**Fourthelerily:** You and yo' nappy-headed sista' clean this house befo' I gets back. Me and my boy is goin' downtown to Higbee's Department Store to get him some new fashionables for school. I'll takes you two on down to the Goodwill for one outfit a piece once yo' welfare checks come in, if (and only if) you get dis house so spotless that I can wipe a white glove across the surfaces and not pick up one speck of dust on my finger. Clean spankability is next to godliness— that's what I always say. Then, and only then, will Goodwill see yo' sorry asses for some garmeting."

The money Burley-pig received from the Welfare Department for two foster children helped supplement her "rich and fabulous" lifestyle which included obscenely wide-brimmed, feather hats worn with tight-fitting garish dresses that barely stretched over her hippo butt. She also acquired two free maids when we were placed in her home, so that she could spend her time being the head gossip of the neighborhood and the queen of her store-front Pentecostal church.

The clothes from Goodwill were always too small (for me), too big (for Pee-wee), or years behind the fashion trend (for both of us). My outfit for the first day of junior high school in 1962 was a pink, felt poodle skirt from the 50s, complete with an appliquéd poodle and chain stitched up the front, with black and white oxfords that were a size too small and had been worn by a person whose left foot had a permanent slew-foot angle of thirty degrees and counting. It was topped off by a dingy red cashmere sweater that was two sizes too small, reeked of the previous owner's rancid body odor, and barely covered my 38-D ta-tas. I was inadvertently sporting a bare mid-drift and muffin top four decades before it would become fashionable. I can still hear the cacophony of laughter as my ill-fitting shoes caused me to helplessly and uncontrollably tack left through the school corridors. I urgently prayed for the Rapture to lift me up to Jesus as I tried to keep from careening into kids like a ship whose mast had come undone.

My foster mother didn't become dangerous to me until she realized I was smart and her son wasn't. My love affair with books happened under her watch and when it did, she turned nasty. If she caught me with a library book, she'd try and make me return it.

If she discovered me doing homework, she'd hide my schoolbooks. When I took to reading under my covers in the middle of the night with a flashlight, she'd stage kamikaze raids to try and catch me. Rowena practically became delirious with excitement when she discovered that making me skip school to punish me for some minor infraction made me physically ill. In retrospect, it was the best thing she could have done to stoke the fire of my lust for learning, because to spite her I went out of my way to study and read, even if it meant getting up in the middle of the night, molding a "pillow body" in the bed, and hiding in the closet with a stolen flashlight to complete my assignments.

※❋※

Burley-pig had never been educated above the sixth grade. She had never read a book for pleasure and could not do basic math or common fractions, but she tried to mask her stupidity with her employers by pretending she had completed high school. At the end of my first year with the Burleys, I called my new caseworker and accused Rowena of attempted murder. She tried to beat me to death with a five-foot lead pipe because of compound fractions and chicken fricassee.

Earlier in the week, Burley-pig had forced me to multiply the fractions of individual recipes into measurements to cover eighty meals for a luncheon at the white lady's house where she worked. Rowena was a good cook, but she made all of her meals from memory. These particular recipes were favorites of the mistress of the house, and when she asked Rowena if she could make them for such a large party, my foster mother assured her employer that it had already been taken care of.

Maybe if Burley-pig had not constantly tried to thwart my education or my love of reading, it would not have crossed my mind to do what I did. My momentary act of rebellious "miscalculation of the fractions" turned the luncheon into a culinary hell that promptly got Burley-pig fired.

When I came home from school that fateful day, my foster mother was sitting in a chair staring at her maid's uniform which was balled up in her lap. For the longest time she said nothing—just stared at me with eyes smoldering with hatred while she twisted the uniform back and forth in between her hands.

"You, you demon . . . I'll kill you, I swear I'll kill you, I swear I'll pummelgate you, even if it is the last thing I do," Burley-pig said as she charged at me with the rage of a pit bull. She shoved me down the basement stairs and started beating me with a lead pipe that was at the bottom of the steps. I was too agile for her and out-maneuvered most of her blows until she stopped from sheer exhaustion.

Burley-pig locked me in the basement for twenty-four hours and made me miss school which was worse than being beaten. Fearing for my life, I called my new caseworker as soon as I could sneak out to a phone. She was young, idealistic, and intuitive, with a freshly minted social worker's degree, and she believed me when I told her that my foster mother was trying to kill me. The new Miss Perkins—the only decent caseworker Pee-wee and I ever had—removed both of us from the Burleys within the week. No place could be found that would take two older kids, so we were sent to separate foster homes. The new Miss Perkins only lasted for six months in her job which meant Pee-wee and I were set adrift in the system. Except for a brief stint in a Colored version of a YWCA for three months, the exodus from Burley-pig's home was the end of our co-existing as sisters in the same foster home for the rest of our childhood journey.

❊❖❊

I am discovering that it would be very helpful if along with a soundtrack, God would provide children in abusive or bullied situations a crystal ball that they could look into to see a point in time when their lives would get better. It wouldn't have to be a ninety-minute Lifetime movie—just a YouTube clip of the abused making the abusers' heads explode in disbelief and wide-eyed envy.

If I had known that someday Pee-wee and I would be able to rub Burley-pig's face in her own shit, I think we would have suffered less in her hands as children.

On one of those rare, sweet, self-indulgent moments in life, my sister and I returned to Cleveland after eighteen years of avoiding our birthplace and showed Rowena Burley just how much she had miscalculated us.

Mama died at age seventy, completely losing her battle with schizophrenia, and Pee-wee and I went back to Cleveland to bury her. We discovered that Burley-pig was one of the deaconesses at the store-front church where my mother's funeral was being held. She still lived in the same Sears and Roebuck pre-fab house, was still cleaning toilets for white folks, and she'd gotten even fatter. Her doted-upon son had become a ne'er-do-well who still lived with her, and her husband was nowhere to be found.

When Pee-wee and I glided into the funeral home like rock stars in our color-coordinated, black and white suits that Pee-wee had designed and made, Burley-pig had purposely placed herself beside Mama's casket. I imagined she did so to gloat. Rowena Burley's jaw dropped to her 48GGG breasts when she saw that we had matured into beautiful black women who sported athletically lean bodies and wore impeccable make-up with stylish Afros of the 70s. The "Rev. Ike" preacher crowed about our college degrees, educational accomplishments, and new careers from the pulpit. The stupefied look on Burley-pig's face was a gift from heaven—a*bsolutely, fucking priceless!* As we laid our mother to rest, Pee-wee and I turned our backs on Rowena Burley as she scampered after us like a lap dog—doing everything in her power to cozy up to us and engage us in conversation. Pee-wee and I smiled at each other, picked up our pace, and left Burley-pig in the dust as we refused to acknowledge her existence in the moment and let go of the fact that she ever had any power to harm us. When I looked over my shoulder to see if we had been able to shake Burley-pig, I saw a pusillanimous old woman lagging behind, gasping for breath, and desperately trying to catch up with my sister and me so that she could boast to the funeral attendees from her church that she had once been our foster mother. *Revenge is, indeed, a dish best served cold!*

10
Get Out Of My Way, Poseidon

~

"There are very few monsters who warrant the fear we have of them."—**André Gide**

Do you know what I've discovered about monsters who think they are all that and a bag of chips? Most of them are posers. If you don't give up in your fight against them, you can eventually kick their asses, outrun them, outsmart them, and be on your way.

❄❄

My cruelest foster father never physically abused me but did his utmost to psychologically devastate me. He was a black man named after a Confedcrate Civil War general: Stonewall Jackson. By the time I entered this nine-parts-cream-one-part-chocolate black man's home, I had become enough of a reader to fully understand the irony of his name, and I didn't hesitate to mutter just loud enough for him to hear: *"Who in the hell names a Negro after a Confederate general who was a slave owner to boot?"*

The Stonewall Jackson who was my foster father was an albino and the descendent of interracial grandparents. His skin had a translucent hue that always looked as if it wanted to reject the host at a moment's notice. He pretended that he was as white as any white person in Cleveland, but he was just "grey." His eyes were almost purple, but he listed them on official forms as blue. Because the thinness of his nose and lips were patterned after his white grandfather rather than his black grandmother, one could mistake him for a white man from a distance. By the time I met him, some underlying auto-immune disease had caused all of his hair to fall out. At least that is what his wife said. I could see the evidence of her claim when I studied Stonewall's bald head, but as to his other hairless parts, I took his wife's word for it.

Stonewall was married to a prominent minister's daughter from New York who was also "fair of skin," and together they took extreme pride in the misguided idea that they were part of Cleveland's black elite. Pee-wee ended up in a similar home in another area of Cleveland, and she would eventually be dumped back into the system because her "high yellow" foster mother felt that Pee-wee was too dark-skinned for her to fit in with their family. So long as my sister did the jobs of a maid and stayed out of sight, she was allowed to live in their Shaker

Heights home. But she and her foster family parted ways when Pee-wee asked to join them on a work picnic for the staff of a man who would eventually become one of Cleveland's first black congressmen. Pee-wee later told me that no white people had ever cut her as deeply as the bigotry of our own people who judged her as unworthy because of the color of her skin.

※❈※

People like Pee-wee's foster parents and the Jacksons belonged to those Negro social clubs of the 1960's that still had cotillions and formal balls. The clubs didn't allow a person membership unless they were the sons and daughters of the Negro upper class (doctors, lawyers, college deans, teachers, politicians, and wealthy business moguls). And even then, people were only included if they passed the paper bag test (having skin color lighter than a brown paper bag). That left me at least two paper-bag degrees on the outside looking in and left poor Pee-wee on another continent.

I first met Mrs. Stonewall Jackson when I was looking for baby-sitting jobs while I was in junior high school. Once she learned that I was a "reasonably intelligent and responsible girl," she promptly hired me as their *au pair*. (These were the Jacksons, for you: all the other Colored folks would have called me a babysitter, but they traveled in a realm where their shit didn't stink, and they wanted you to know it.)

As an *au pair* living outside their home, I got along fine with them although I secretly considered them to be a Negro version of Dickens' Mr. Bumble and Mrs. Corney. Mrs. Stonewall was petite and rather pretty, but she was a silly woman. Her raison d'être was being the wife of a wealthy man with a lifestyle she could flaunt before the rest of the black community. She displayed her largesse by employing me, a "poor black child." On the other hand, Mr. Stonewall was extremely smart, aloof, and completely put off by the sufferings of anybody but himself, and he wanted no part of the "reach back and help his race" gig unless it profited him in some way. But if the truth be known, for a while I worshipped the ground they walked on because here were black people who lived like white people—a world free of ignorance and want. When Stonewall commanded that I "jump," I'd respond with military immediacy: *"Yes sir. How high, sir?"*

I had never seen Negroes like this. They were rich. Mrs. Stonewall wore fur coats, pearls, and beautiful clothes purchased from upscale department stores. I had finally found people that I thought could point me in the direction of a better life—the way life was meant to be—and I was as anxious to get to know them as they were to flaunt their wealth and social status before me.

※※

Life has a funny way of exposing the fraud behind the curtain. The year I was kicked out of foster home number "five-thousand-and-ten" Mr. and Mrs. Stonewall Jackson enthusiastically came to the rescue. But living with them confirmed a very, very, valuable lesson about life: *if it sounds too good to be true—trust me—it really is too good to be true.* The moment I crossed the threshold to take up residence as a foster child, the verbal abuse and the second-class citizenship began. I foolishly expected parents, and they were expecting a live-in maid who was to be seen but never heard.

In the beginning, I was happy to do anything if it meant I could be a part of their glittery orbit. But no matter what I did, it was never good enough, talented enough, intelligent enough, fast enough, or light-skinned enough. I was never allowed to attend their social gatherings as a member of their family because I wasn't "anything" enough. I once made six A's on my report card—with one B+ in gym (I could never climb that damn rope)—and I got inducted into the National Honor Society and Cleveland's All-City Choir. But after seeing my report card, all Master Stonewall could say was: "So what happened with your grade in gym? You've got to be stupid not to be able to get an 'A' in gym."

The moment I knew all hope was lost of ever belonging to the Jackson family was the day I lost control of the orange juice. Because I never knew when I was going to be publically humiliated by him for some perceived infraction of his 1,001 OCD rules, I had become a nervous wreck. While I lived with him I developed a very visible tic in my right eye, and my hands shook whenever I came into Stonewall's presence. This, and everything else about me, annoyed the hell out of Stonewall Jackson.

As I was serving breakfast to his children one morning, I picked up the orange juice container to pour some into their glasses. At that moment my foster father walked into the kitchen and brushed past me, and the entire bottle slipped from my quivering hands—spilling all over the counter and onto the floor. I watched as the orange color splashed all over Stonewall's pristine business suit and spread across the kitchen floor like the first rays of sunlight rapidly fanning out across the horizon.

In that one defining moment, I knew without a doubt my tenure with the uppity Negroes had come to an end. I was speechless as the Earth stopped turning, and the tableau of wife, children, and terrified foster child froze waiting for the inevitable Stonewall berating. He turned his back on me and issued his verdict about my character and future to his wife in barely more than a clenched whisper. "I could care less whether she comes or goes, lives or dies; if she were my child I would care, but since she's not and never could be, just get her out of my sight." In that one dismissive moment, Stonewall duplicated the same disappointment that the absentee Mail Carrier had taken years to accomplish.

※※

Just because someone is horrid, self-centered, and cruel, and their behavior makes you feel like pond scum, that doesn't mean one can't learn from them. On one of the vacation trips I took with the Jacksons as their *au pair* before the great orange juice explosion, their babies were having a hard time falling asleep in the back of the station wagon as we drove through the night toward a cabin in Maine. I began to sing lullabies to the children that were spirituals I grew up hearing Mama sing. It wasn't something I thought about at the time, and I certainly never considered myself a singer—it was just a natural response to a need.

The singing was effective, and as I settled back down to read one of my proverbial books, I heard Stonewall whisper to his wife: "Who knew she had any talent?"

"I certainly didn't know," responded Mrs. Uppity Nigger. "Maybe we should tell her about the Settlement House for music."

"I'm not paying for her to have music lessons," said Stonewall.

"Maybe they'll give her a scholarship," replied Mrs. SJ.

"Well, if pigs had wings, wishes would fly, now wouldn't they?" said Mr. Asshole Foster Father.

But I had ears even if I didn't have wings. I sat very still and listened very carefully, and I felt a shift in the currents of my life as I reiterated the name of the music school to myself over and over again. Somehow, I knew that the parents from Hell had just opened the door to a new world by inadvertently admitting that I had talent.

※❀※

Homer made sure Odysseus had Telemachus, the cow-herd, and the swineherd to help him kick the asses of his rivals. God gave me an opera singer, a high school principal, a head clerk, and the wife of a dead college president to help me slay my enemies.

※❀※

The day I auditioned for the Settlement House I met The Opera Singer who became my vocal teacher for two years. She was the first white person that I ever got to know as an individual, and she told me I could sing—*really sing*. She wanted to be my teacher and open up the world of classical music to me. When I told her I had no money to pay her for lessons, she laughed and said, "Who asked you for money?"

Even though I didn't know where Middle C was on the piano, my voice teacher convinced me that I had a voice that could someday sing the works of Menotti, Puccini, and Rachmaninoff—whoever they were. When she personally introduced me to Leonard Bernstein and helped secure me an understudy role in **Amahl and the Night Visitors** that the Maestro was conducting in Cleveland, I thought I had died and gone to Heaven. And when my angel secured a place for me in one of the best music summer camps in the nation to study opera for two months, I knew Pipsqueak's ship was comin' in!

※❀※

I am discovering that when we look back over our lives after we've lived a good many years, sometimes we can see when the fairy dust first begins to be sprinkled on our destinies. It's ever so slight, but if we stop and take notice, we'll usually see a rainbow in the distance, too.

11

Ignorance And Want

~

"They are Man's and they cling to me, appealing from their fathers. This boy is Ignorance and this girl is Want. Beware them both, and all of their degree, but most of all beware this boy for on his brow I see that written which is Doom, unless the writing be erased." — **A Christmas Carol,** by Charles Dickens,

Do you know what I've discovered? The South didn't have a corner on the market when it came to Jim Crow laws. White folks in northern cities like Cleveland, Ohio had all sorts of things they tried to keep Black folks from enjoying as they locked the doors of segregation on us and tried to throw away the keys. But in the mid-sixties a tidal wave of protests *("Hell no, segregation must go—Hell yes, education's our quest!")* was emerging, and a small band of angels would teach Pee-wee and me how to surf that wave out of ignorance and want.

※❋※

In 1965 Cleveland was a racist cesspool. It had a conglomerate of white groups from various areas of the city aggressively united to block Black folks from working, living, and getting educated on the same level that they and their children enjoyed. It created a perfect storm for black minds to be wasted, souls to be crushed, and destinies to be derailed. But the Civil Rights Movement was moving full steam ahead and the Cleveland governmental agencies were forced to bow to the pressure of the Civil Rights Act of 1964 and to the collective black voices in our city who demanded a better education for their children. As a result, the school board capitulated by building more schools to try and alleviate the overcrowding and segregation in the predominantly black areas of the East Side of Cleveland.

After I found my voice teacher and right before I got kicked out of the Jacksons' home, I was allowed to enroll in a brand new, state-of-the-art high school. It straddled the border of the middle-class black neighborhood the Jacksons' had moved from and the fringe area of the suburb that whites were begrudgingly abandoning to middle-class blacks. Theoretically, my high school was supposed to draw attendance equally from both sides of the color line. The Cleveland Board of

Education had selected some of their best black and white teachers for this premier school to show it was putting its best foot forward. It also hired a man who would become one of Cleveland's first black principals of what was supposed to be a racially-balanced high school. But before the school opened, "white flight" hit that school's neighborhoods like the scattering of sandpipers fleeing a fast-approaching wave. We ended up with a high school made up of approximately ninety-five percent black students with a few white students who couldn't move as quickly as their cohorts had, but who snuck out to safer pastures as soon as they could manage it.

Some of the white teachers had not counted on working for a black principal or teaching at a predominantly black school, but the ones who didn't just up and quit joined a group of outstanding black teachers and guidance counselors to form the visionary crew of an amazing ship designed to sail as many black kids as possible through a crack in the wall of ignorance and out onto the seas of opportunity. Enrolling in this high school and embracing the educational excellence that the principal demanded was another building block, in addition to books and music, that would help me escape the inevitability to which I had been born. Another was being kicked to the curb by the Cleveland Welfare System.

※◈※

"Eleanor, I requested that you come see me today because, as you know, you're being asked to leave the Jacksons' home due to an insubordinate attitude and behavioral problems," said barely-able-to-contain-her-ennui-caseworker-Miss-Perkins-number-two-hundred-and-counting. She didn't even bother to look at me when she delivered my fate.

"In all honesty, we have nowhere else to place you because the Court no longer has responsibility for its wards once they've turned sixteen. However, we have some terrific news for you [still not looking at me—not even once]. We have decided to provide a stipend for you to rent a room at a boarding facility that is kind of like a Colored Women's YWCA for homeless women. We'll pay your rent and give you one meal ticket a day until you're eighteen. (You'll have to provide the other two meals, somehow.) It has been decided since you are an articulate Colored person we can help get you a job at the telephone company as a switchboard operator. That should give you what you need for bus fare, clothing, and incidentals."

"No," I said, barely able to breathe.

"What do you mean, 'no'?" asked the current Miss Perkins, who finally deigned to look up.

"NO as in N-O! I want to stay in school. You didn't say anything about staying in school. I have two more years before I graduate," I said.

"And do what? You can legally leave school at sixteen and given your prospects, getting out of school now, and getting a secure job is nothing to sneeze at. As a Colored girl, whether you leave school now or two years from now, the outcome will be the same. Now, I'm not asking you, I'm telling you."

"HELL, NO! I make all A's. You can't do this to me. Have you even bothered to check my report cards or talk to my teachers or my principal?"

"I don't need to check with your school about this decision, because according to the aptitude test you took with Human Services last month, you scored only two points above the retardation level—technically, some employers would consider you retarded. You should be grateful I can get you a job at the telephone company, and you don't have to become a domestic."

"ARE YOU A FUCKING IDIOT, OR WHAT?" I said. "It wasn't my fault that I did so badly on your stupid test. They left me in a room with a guy who kept messing with me—he kept trying to feel me up and steal my purse. I can't take it when people mess with me; I couldn't concentrate." As I started to panic, I started throwing everything I could find in my school book bag at her. "What retarded person has **A Tale of Two Cities** in her book bag to read (just for fun!), and a German language test that I've just aced? Look at this test. Can you see that big fat 'A' at the top of the page?"

"That's not the point. . . ."

"That is the fucking point! I'm going to talk to my voice teacher; she won't let this happen to me.

She says I have a real talent for music, and if I stay in school I might be able to become a performer; so I'M STAYING IN SCHOOL, YOU CRACKER BITCH!"

The fury on my caseworker's face was so intense she couldn't speak, but it was outstripped by the fury emanating from mine. If it hadn't been for a case-worker-in-training who sat in on the meeting, I think the current Miss Perkins and I would have killed each other with our bare hands. I know it was the junior-Miss-Perkins-in-training who saved my destiny.

Before any cataclysmic decisions were made, Miss Perkins-in-training timidly volunteered that she'd wit-nessed the incident of the molester/thief during the testing. She acknowledged that I had become very upset, and it probably affected my test scores. That input made the current CW storm out of the room with CW-in-training scurrying behind her. After what seemed like an eternity, a more senior CW came into the room and announced that I could stay in school. However, that would cut me off from any financial support they could offer except for a stipend for rent at the Colored Women's home. I would need to find a way to support, feed, and clothe myself. In other words, I would need to work and attend school at the same time.

I guess they figured that would never hap-pen, and I'd come crawling back to the Cleveland Welfare Department to follow their advice. God bless President John F. Kennedy and his federally-funded work programs, started for the sole purpose of help-ing mentally retarded and poor Colored children fin-ish high school.

❈❈❈

The day I entered my high school's office to apply for a job as a typist, I met The Head Clerk. She worked for The Principal. Together they led an office staff that supported the teachers and the students. The Head Clerk was a black woman in her mid-thirties who didn't countenance fools and took no prisoners. I was told that The Principal refused to take the job of leading an integrated school without her by his side. The Head Clerk was one formidable black woman, and even the white teachers were afraid to face her if she called them on the carpet for some administrative infraction.

I entered the school office fifteen minutes late. I had on my best Goodwill outfit, and I was struttin'. Trying to keep up with the new mini-skirt fashion, I had taken a one-size-too-small purple skirt and rolled it up at the waist. The hem fell about six inches above my chunky-body-pig-knuckle knees. Like a two-scoop ice-cream cone, I had topped off the skirt with a faded, tight-fitting cashmere sweater. My second-hand shoes had folded scraps of newspapers inside cover-ing the holes in the soles, and my ham-bone thighs were proudly encased in black fish-net stockings. I just knew I was hot stuff as my undulating red-lipstick mouth aggressively popped two sticks of Juicy Fruit gum loud enough to be heard in Philadelphia.

Obviously sporting a death wish, I introduced myself with over-the-top impertinence, "Hey Lady, are you The Head Clerk?"

A regal, stately, black woman—who could have easily been the Queen of England in an alternate universe—turned to look at me with an unfazed, royal stare. She said absolutely nothing as I continued to aggressively pop my gum. At that High Noon moment, like a fool, I got pissed that she wasn't answering me, and I drew my verbal pistol: "Listen, I'm here to get a job, but I can't wait around all day. Do you or don't you have a job for me, woman?"

The Head Clerk didn't bother to respond but continued to look at me with an intensity that I had never experienced in my entire life and would never experience from anybody else again. Her face held no anger nor animosity, no arrogance nor disdain—just a calculated moral assessment of my entire shoddy character as her eyes pierced straight through to my soul.

"What is your name, young lady?"

Sullenly, I stared back at her and slowly answered: "Eleanor Maxwell."

"Well, Miss Maxwell, we'll have to see about that," The Head Clerk said. She had a kind and level tone that would never change by one note in the entire time that I would come to know her.

"My name is Mrs. M, and if you expect to work for me you'll always address me as such—not 'hey lady' and certainly not 'woman.' In the meantime, you'll remove that wad of gum, throw it in the trash behind you and never enter this office again with anything in your mouth other than your teeth and your tongue. Third, you'll wipe off that red lipstick because it is not appropriate for this office nor is it appropriate for your age.

"Finally, that sweater and skirt are much too tight and too short for your figure. You will need to dress more appropriately if you wish to work in a professional environment. A simple skirt and blouse will be more conducive, and if you don't have these articles of clothing, I will make arrangements to get you the proper attire.

"Furthermore, tardiness is not an option: I will expect you promptly at 7:30 a.m. each school day, then again during all study hall periods, and immediately after the closing bell. Once your office assignments are done, you'll go into the back room and do your homework. If you can abide by these few simple rules, Miss Maxwell, when I am finished with you, you'll be able to get a secretarial job any place in the country because I plan to teach you *more* than how to type a letter—I plan to teach you how to carry yourself like a dignified Woman of Color. I'm told that you're smart, and I believe you have the ability to be whatever you want to be on this Earth, but you won't get there by being rude and crude. Am I making myself clear, Miss Maxwell?"

God, this woman pissed me off. But I needed that job; so for the first time in my life, I shut my mouth and acquiesced to every rule The Head Clerk threw at me.

⁂

The Head Clerk had a confidence about her that defied the times, and for the next two years she utilized that confidence along with grace and mercy to guide me. This amazing black woman of modest financial means took me to affordable stores or acquired used clothing and shoes from her wealthier friends to help me obtain outfits that showed me at my best. She checked my homework, made sure I had completed my assignments, and course-corrected my behavior when I stepped out of line.

As our relationship grew beyond employer-employee to mentor-mentee, The Head Clerk became my life coach. She took me to restaurants and showed me how to eat with the proper utensils and to theaters to experience the beauty of the written word fleshed out on stage. As the Civil Rights Movement unfolded across the country and barriers began to break down in Cleveland, she became driven about taking me to places she said the "white folks had been keeping from us." My Sojourner Truth implanted the concept in me that the world was my oyster; nothing could stop me from becoming a pearl—absolutely nothing—except fear and misplaced anger.

❉❉

It was The Head Clerk's quick thinking that kept me from getting expelled and sent to jail for an act that was inevitable given the circumstances and my growing anger due to my childhood abuse. When a white teacher at my high school started to verbally assault an entire class of black students and me in particular, I went ballistic. She insulted the class by declaring us "incapable of learning." Teaching us, she declared, "was a giant waste of her time."

I came undone. Before I even knew what I was doing, I picked up my chair and bolted to the front of the class to beat the shit out of that ignorant woman. All the anger, all the tears, all the rejection, all the misery, all the numerous CWs' attempts to thwart my education, and all the hatred for everyone who had caused me harm culminated in that one moment, and I didn't care about anything or anyone. I'm not in prison today because two of my male classmates diverted my attack. They intercepted me and dragged me, kicking and screaming, to the office and into the charge of The Head Clerk.

The Head Clerk hid me in a locked filing-room and told me not to move or make a sound until she came to get me. At the end of the school day, after everyone had left the building, she let me out of the room and told me I wouldn't have any more problems with my teacher because she had taken care of the situation.

"But, young lady, if you try and kill everyone who insults you, as a black woman you won't get past next week without ending up in jail. Being able to shoulder disrespect is a cross all Black folks have to bear with grace. It isn't what white folks say about you, it's what you believe in your heart about yourself that matters. The next time you feel like killing someone, I suggest that would be a good time to take a walk and have a little talk with Jesus. Do you understand what I'm telling you, child?"

I returned to class the next day and it was as if nothing had happened. The teacher couldn't look me in the eyes for a long, long time, but she never messed with me or any of her other black students again. From that day forward I became convinced The Head Clerk not only walked on water but she wasn't afraid of anyone or anything. And I knew that more than anything—I wanted to be like her.

❊❊❊

The Opera Singer was the first person to agree with The Head Clerk and The Principal that I should go to college. "Times are changing and integration doors are opening at colleges," they practically said in unison as they all hunted for ways to gather money for me to take that step. The Miss Perkins of the "quit-school-at-sixteen" throwdown tried to thwart my merry band of warriors, but they held strong against her by fighting her with weapons of faith in me: "Eleanor is graduating with honors and at the top of her class—she is going to college whether you like it or not. Go away—you're outnumbered here."

My voice teacher inadvertently found the way for me to attend college when she appeared as a soloist for a performance at a large, exclusively white church one auspicious Sunday morning. At the end of the service an old white lady approached her with an odd request: "I am the widow of the president of a small liberal arts college, and I am interested in helping to fund the education of a poor, black, female vocalist. Would you happen to know of such a person?"

※❀※

In the fall of 1967, after a stern pep talk from The Principal about being a credit to my race and all, The Head Clerk and Pee-wee drove me to my liberal arts college with a trunk full of new clothes made by my sister. The Opera Singer had drilled a basic music repertoire into my head, and I set sail like the young man in the Thomas Cole painting, *Voyage of Life: Youth*—eyes on the illusive prize in the sky while ignorant of the river's trajectory and impending rapids below.

Three months before I left for college, Pee-wee got kicked out of her "high-yellow" foster home for existing while black. She asked the current Miss Perkins not to send her to another foster home but to allow her to live at the Women's Center for the summer with me. Pee-wee requested she be given the same independent living deal to finish high school that I'd had, and with the help of The Principal and The Head Clerk, they fixed a transfer for her to my high school so that they could try and rescue her as they had me.

After I went off to college, the petite sixteen-year-old Pee-wee traveled to high school on two buses from her solitary room at the Women's Center that contained a bed, a sink, a desk, and a chair (bathrooms were down the hall). She took my old job in the school office under the tutelage of The Head Clerk and The Principal. Pee-wee told me years later that on the first day of school The Principal greeted her with a rhetorical question, and a declaration that made her shake from head to toe: "You're Eleanor's sister, aren't you? I expect you to follow in her footsteps and do as well or better. The Head Clerk and I are watching you."

Pee-wee, who I am convinced channeled the spirit of Aunt Lily, became a superb designer and seamstress, and she developed a reputation as one of those rare creatures who could create original patterns out of paper bags, newspapers, and just plain air. During Pee-wee's senior year she entered one of her formal gown creations (hand-stitched with 3,000 beads from waist to hem) into a *Vogue* contest for high school seniors. She won first prize, but The Head Clerk, The Principal, and the guidance counselors were stumped as to how to parlay that into a college education.

Several months after winning the Vogue contest, a college recruiter got stuck at the Cleveland airport during a bad snow storm. He had failed in his attempt to secure any female candidates for his all-male, all-white Textile and Science College in another state. As he was perusing one of the Cleveland newspapers, he saw an advertisement for a job fair at our high school. The recruiter called my high school from the airport, and Pee-wee just happened to be the telephone operator on deck that day who patched him over to The Head Clerk who in turn conferenced in the guidance counselor.

"I just saw the ad for your job fair," said the stranded recruiter. "I know this may sound like an odd question, but is it remotely possible that you might have a talented, female student who has an interest in textile, science, and design?" The Head Clerk said: "We only have one that fits that description, and I'm looking at her. But she will need a full scholarship, money for incidentals, and two plane tickets home a year."

Pee-wee became part of the first freshmen class of women and minorities to break the color and gender barrier at her college, and when she did, we would both wipe the dust of Cleveland off our feet, returning only to bury our mother eighteen years later.

I am discovering that forces on a micro and macro level—beyond our control—mess with our lives night and day, and they can be frustrating as hell. In the world of Ignorance and Want miracles are not frequent, but when they do happen, it is best to grab hold of them with all our might and let them take us where they will as they erase the Doom once written upon our foreheads.

12

On The Other Side Of The Looking Glass

~

"When the Star-Belly children
went out to play ball,
Could a Plain Belly get in the game. . .?
Not at all.
You only could play if your bellies
had stars
And the Plain Belly children had none upon
thars. "
— *by Dr.Seuss from* **The Sneetches**

Do you know what I've discovered? Just because someone sends you an invitation to attend a party doesn't mean the other guests will agree to dance with you.

❋❋

"Oh fuck, I'm going to die—I know it, I know it, I know it!" I muttered to myself.

There I was with my 200-pound, thigh-rubbing, knee-knocking body shivering my ass off in the middle of the night, in the middle of the campus commons with the rest of the Black Student Union—completely surrounded by policemen in riot gear who were poised and ready to shoot my black ass into kingdom come. So I did what any novice militant would do in my circumstance: *I shat my pants.* In response to my terrorized bowels, I dropped two bags full of fried chicken dripping with Crisco all over my feet, and I started to shake uncontrollably.

"God, if I get out of this alive, I swear to you—I SWEAR TO YOU—I'll resign my official position as chief cook for the revolution and find out why in the hell you really put my sorry ass on this planet."

❈❈

I loved being in college. *I especially loved that college.* It truly was one of the places white folks had been keeping from us. Many of the other black students complained about its overwhelming "whiteness" and being in the middle of nowhere, but I thought it was a beautiful campus and couldn't believe I was being paid to go somewhere "just to learn." There were no roaches, no rats, no perverts, and no filth. Every Friday night was "steak night," and I could study everything from

English Literature to archery. Having never before set foot outside of Cleveland, when it was all said and done, my alma mater afforded me the opportunity to sing my way across much of the United States as well as many European countries.

I had won a scholarship to one of the best liberal arts schools in the nation. Because of its religious history and affiliation, it was a school that really wanted to do the right thing. But wanting and doing is a whole different ballgame, and this well-meaning, but naïve educational enclave didn't know what in the hell to do with the handful of black students it recruited and wooed to its campus in the fall of 1967. We weren't many, but we were enough to compel some white parents to withdraw their children, and others declared: "My child's not rooming with a nigger." There were more than enough protests to quickly motivate the Dean of Women to move the three black female freshmen in together to share one dorm room in order to muffle the uproar. The Dean had idealistically thought if she randomly placed the three black women in my freshmen class amongst our white dorm mates, we'd all learn to bloom together and form a harmonious garden. Much had been done to meet their "brown quota" in response to the Civil Rights Act of 1964, but little had been done to bridge the gap in racial attitudes that persisted.

As an Affirmative Action baby I was a voice major who, though I had only known where middle 'C' was on the piano for a couple of years, boldly declared Piano as my minor. I was so Affirmative Action that when I auditioned for my vocal scholarship, I had laryngitis. I couldn't sing a goddamn note that day, but they accepted me anyway. (The music department took The Opera Singer's word for it that I had vocal talent.) Dissertation-like papers were due in English, religion, and music history. Formal recitals were expected in voice and piano at the end of each semester. A basic proficiency was required in all sections of the orchestral family, and math was being taught on a level only Einstein could comprehend—or so it seemed to me.

It isn't that I wasn't vocally talented or intellectually strong, it's just that in the process of trying to survive, I had not acquired the skill set needed to compete against kids who had learned to play Chopin at six, read Dostoevsky at ten, and who hadn't spent their developmental years living under a reign of terror. I had entered an uncharted world without a roadmap or a compass, and in spite of my excellent high school experience with my merry band of warriors supporting me, the rest of my schooling had been piss-poor and had left me with gaping holes in my education. I knew I was drowning, and drowning fast, but I couldn't let that stop me from trying to swim the channel. Besides, I would have accepted a scholarship in Sumo wrestling for leprechauns at a Hebrew university on the moon if it meant escaping Cleveland

and getting an education.   I did what I'd always done in life—I forged full-speed ahead and hoped no one would notice I didn't know a damn thing about what I was doing.

※※

The English Professor was my Freshman Comp 101 teacher and probably the only Jew on the staff of this overtly Protestant college. He was short in stature and could have been the twin of Groucho Marx. After a couple months of witnessing me try to tread water, he called me into his office and offered me a life raft.

"Are you interested in making it here, Miss Maxwell?"

I didn't know what to say so I just nodded my head and tried not to cry, realizing I might have made a mistake and should have followed my caseworker's order to drop out of school at sixteen and become a telephone operator.

"It is obvious you have talent, Miss Maxwell, but you've never heard of the infinitive which is why you don't recognize when you split it, and you don't have a clue as to how a college paper should be constructed. But if you allow me to tutor you outside of class, I guarantee that you will sail through your next four years. I would very much like to see you succeed, Miss Maxwell, because I know what it's like to be a fish out of water. But I warn you, if you do not accept my offer

I predict you won't make it past your freshman year. It's up to you."

"Got it!" I cried. "Where do I find a butt-load of other teachers like you because English isn't the only subject that's kicking my ass?"

I eventually met two other professors who became my personal guides through the system, and this husband-wife team was one of the major reasons I not only completed my musical requirements but even made the Dean's List. The Music Professor was a prematurely balding, moderately famous concert pianist. His Wife, whose stately carriage was as full of grace as it was full of classical talent, had been an opera singer in New York. Together they exuded warmhearted color-blindness and opened up their home to me. The Wife especially championed me and saved my butt more than once in those tumultuous years.

Not every teacher thought I deserved to be there. I had been harshly schooled in taking the temperature of my own people, but reading the nuances of this white world was beyond my scope. Repressed by the religious culture in which they taught and the small town environment in which they lived, many of my professors danced a complicated tango by saying what they didn't mean, living what they didn't believe, and closeting who they truly were.

I got used to The Band Director who could barely contain his contempt for my presence in his marching band and managed to reach his personal best by not speaking one word to me during my entire four years on campus. Of course his problem with me might have been that I couldn't play even one single musical instrument, and yet I had been thrust into his marching band. The Band Director determined within the first week of my arrival that the only instruments I was qualified to play were the cymbals. I would have challenged his decision if I'd known what slamming the cymbals together would mean to my poor body. Each time I raised the heavy metal plates over my head and crashed them together with gusto, I would accidently crush one or both of my humongous breasts between them, and the pain would drop me to my knees in mid-formation during the middle of a game. Whatever his reasons—whether of a musical or a personal nature—The Band Director just pretended I didn't exist and had his teaching assistants relay his instructions to me if he needed to communicate anything at all.

The Theater Director, an unusually homely man, never got used to me. I got used to his sarcasm and lack of warmth, but not to the favoritism he showered on our male lead. The Lead, who fancied himself a reincarnation of Adonis, was always late for rehearsals and caused the rest of the cast to have to wait around until he deigned to show up. One day I got pissed off and told Mr. Adonis to get his act together because my time was valuable. Later, The Theater Director cornered me in an isolated hallway and threatened my future at the school if I didn't mind my own fucking business. At that moment I realized he was screwing The Lead. This was definitely not considered permissible at my religious college. Whether because of my race or my gender, it was clear I wasn't ever going to be one of his favorites.

But these two teachers were lightweights compared to The Head of the Music Department who was also my choir director. When he assigned me a mid-term paper, I chose a modern art song writer and diarist as my topic because I wanted to know what made this musical genius tick and why his music touched me so deeply. Since arriving at college, I had fallen in love with this particular musician's works, and I pulled together my newfound writing skills and my lust for learning to write what I intended to be the research paper of my college career. Finding nothing in my Christian college library except musical rank and file statistics on this composer, I took a trip back to Cleveland and, after searching through several downtown bookstores, I found a wealth of material that revealed the psyche of the man in his own words: **The Paris Diary of Ned Rorem (1966)** and **The New York Diary of Ned Rorem (1967).**

I'd never read anything like Rorem's books. In his diaries, Ned Rorem revealed himself to be narcissistic and arrogant as hell, a staunch atheist, and brutally honest about himself and everyone else. He had a Churchill-type acerbic wit, was a seemingly insatiable alcoholic for a season, and was unapologetically gay before it was cool to be gay. His antics and his lifestyle were somewhat foreign to me, but I was awed by his honesty, touched by his pain, and entranced by his brilliant wit and writing (if and when I understood them since reading his diaries necessitated the constant companionship of a French-English dictionary). I was intrigued by what I surmised were the motivations for the melancholia that ebbed and flowed in Rorem's music. Armed with my newfound writing skills, my Intro to Psychology class notes, and a passionate love for my subject, I wrote what I considered to be an homage to a great musician—warts and all.

❈❈

I failed to notice that The Choir Director's son, who assisted him from time to time, had boasted to anyone who would listen that Ned Rorem was a personal friend of his. Whether this was true or not, he committed the sin of omission when it came to Mr. Rorem's sexuality. While traveling on a choir tour, somewhere between North Carolina and Florida, in the middle of the night when everyone else was asleep, The Choir Director demanded I come to the back of the bus to discuss a matter of grave importance. He and The Son were sitting in the middle of the back bench. As I approached them, I noticed my research paper (who could mistake the proud purple cover I'd encased it in?) was rolled up and mangled in The Son's hand and was being used to punctuate the air between the two of them as if it were a conductor's baton on crack. What I didn't immediately notice was how enraged they both were until the son proceeded to castigate me in his abnormally high-pitched voice about the "multitudinous lies you have written about my famous friend, Ned."

In between The Son's high-pitched cadences of "lies, lies, I tell you," and The Choir Director's screeches of "on whose authority did you write this libel," they practically levitated as they both escalated to a unified verbal crescendo: "WHO DO YOU THINK YOU ARE—BLASPHEMING THIS BRILLIANT MAN?" As groggy chorus members began to stir and turn around in their seats to see what all the commotion was about, The Son growled his final strangled attack: "When you first submitted your mid-term subject, my father and I were going to send it to my famous friend Ned to show him how young Negroes were aspiring to sing his great music. But we wouldn't dare let him see this trash now, you, you, ignorant . . ."

As I waited for the inevitable unspoken nigger punch to slip into the Scrabble word play between The Choir Director's son and me, I stared at my rolled up paper with my college future crushed within it and wondered if I had met the first white people on the planet who didn't read and thought the word "diary" was a synonym for fiction.

Completely shaken, I retreated to my baseline safeguard of being Pipsqueak. I rolled my head in my best black girl kiss-my-ass stance, and with all the courage I had left and all the faith I could muster in the written word of Mr. Rorem, I answered my appalled accusers with what I hoped had more power in it than what I actually felt. *"The man wrote it; I read it and quoted it, which means you better believe it. Besides, Junior, why do you care? You got something to hide?"* I sashayed my fat ass back to my seat at the front of the bus muttering "fuckin' assholes" under my breath, but everything in me was shaking with the knowledge that I had probably killed my illusive rise out of the ghetto and completely annihilated my music scholarship.

I expected to be tossed to the lions after we returned to campus but quite the opposite happened: I got a 'B' in the class, an 'A' in Concert Choir, and I even performed four songs of Rorem's in my final recital. The Son faded out of my life as quickly as he had appeared. No one ever mentioned my research paper on Rorem again. All I can deduce is that The Choir Director must have read the books I had referenced in my paper, and that finally broke down the closet door behind which his son had been hiding.

But The Choir Director's pretentiousness and self-denial weren't the only issues between us. Somewhere between Chapel Hill, North Carolina and Jacksonville, Florida, I discovered he had secretly telegraphed our hosts at the other end that the choir included three Negroes who required "special" housing. The revelation that this little religious school was merely playing at inclusion and acceptance made me all too aware that it would only be a matter of time before another shoe would drop.

❈❖❈

"What's wrong with her?" asked one perfectly coiffed, pink-infused, Chanel-smelling white girl to another, as they passed me convulsing in tears in the dorm hallway while on their way to a Tri-Delta sorority meeting.

"Oh, nothing—one of their people died," said the blonde friend with bored disdain.

As I crumbled to the floor in grief, I remember thinking the hopes and dreams of every black person in America had just been blown away on a balcony in Memphis, but it never caused those white girls to miss a beat in their perfectly pain-free lives as they strutted past me to attend a party at their sorority house. This courageous man, who meant so much to so many, wasn't even worth a moment's thought to those girls or my college in general. Martin Luther King's life and leadership had become like a passport into this all-white world where I didn't quite know all the rules. He had inspired many of us to step through the looking glass and enter a world where we weren't made to feel that we belonged. With Martin's death, suddenly things got a whole lot scarier in my world. Every conversation with a white classmate became an odd dance that exposed a racist underbelly too blatant to ignore.

I'm not saying I didn't have some white friends; it's just that I didn't fit in comfortably with either the white or the black students. I had grown up in a world mostly devoid of whites, and all the middle-class black students came from lives I had only dreamt about. Except for one black friend, who ironically could pass for white, my fellow students never really knew me, and I never fully figured out how to be myself in either group.

If I was with my black friends (kids from parents who were preachers, lawyers, accountants, teachers, and decent mothers and fathers), I pretended to return to holiday-rich family traditions while actually fanaticizing about their summer, Christmas, and Easter vacations. While they did the black Norman Rockwell scenario, I languished in Cleveland's Women's Center with Pee-wee counting the days until I could return to their orbit after school resumed.

With my white friends, I'd share made-up life stories to match their carefree existences ("Oh yes, Daddee and I so enjoy a trip to Cedar Point every now and then."). I'd hang out in their dorm rooms laughing and chatting up a storm or visit their families with them for a quick weekend, and would almost feel at home in the fantasy until one of them would forget I was black.

"Do you want some nuts, Eleanor? I've got cashews, peanuts, and nigger toes. . . ."

Uh, oh.

"Who wants the last cookie Mother sent? I only have one, and there are four of us, so to be perfectly fair I'll choose the winner without any bias. 'Eeny, meeny, miny, moe, catch a nigger by his toe, if he hollars, let him go; Eeny, meeny, miny, moe.'"

Oh goodie, I guess I win!

※❀※

On the night of the campus take-over, I couldn't get over how uneasy I felt about the motivating factors behind the event because they came suddenly and out of nowhere. Every black student on campus was flipping out over the recent hate mail against us that had suddenly appeared in the school newspaper. There were burning crosses outside our dorms, and a Molotov cocktail was thrown into the window of one of the black student's rooms. We huddled together in fear from what we perceived as a campus receiving marching orders from the Ku Klux Klan. It broke my heart that the administration seemed to be deaf, dumb, and blind to what was happening to this segment of its student population. I couldn't escape the nagging feeling I needed to freeze frame the scene and step out of it for a few minutes to sort the truth from the lies. Something didn't add up.

The Black Student Union (BSU) had agreed that even though the racists weren't playing games, we wouldn't exacerbate the issue by bringing any weapons into the situation. That decision probably saved our lives. It would be just a "peaceful sit-in" to make our grievances known—to wake up a clueless administration and campus. We wanted to declare: "We're human, we're here, and what are you going to do about the evil in our midst that is attacking us?" The massacre of white students at Kent State and black students at Jackson State were still national headlines. We were afraid, but we weren't going to sit still while the bigots in our midst publicly challenged our right to an education. Martin Luther King and others had opened the door—we weren't going to let ignorant white folks slam it closed on us again.

❊❂❊

After it was all said and done (the policemen in riot gear that completely surrounded us, the rifles aimed at our heads, and the soiled underwear), some of the black students either got kicked out, dropped out, or accelerated their graduation dates to distance themselves from a place they had grown to despise. I would be one of the black students the administration didn't kick out because my grades were high (I made the Dean's List that year), and what could they accuse me of, anyway: Fried-chicken-carrying-revolutionary-couldn't-control-her-bowels-when-she-thought-she-was-going-to-die-while-surrounded-by-firing-squad? But I still couldn't shake my suspicions that something was off.

A year later, I found out what had really gone on that night, and it turned out to be pure, unadulterated betrayal by one of the BSU leadership and a cover-up by the school administration. The campus takeover was a setup by one of the BSU leaders (a Huey Newton wannabe) who had been manipulated by a couple of white SDS (Students for a Democratic Society) radicals from another college. It's true there were plenty of racists on the faculty, amongst the student body, and in the surrounding towns who had been very vocal about their disdain towards the black students on campus, and the administration *seemed* indifferent to it all. But the radicals who infiltrated our campus after the Kent State massacre were upper-class white militants who had taken an oath to spread anarchy across the USA via college campuses and universities, and they didn't give a flying fuck about the black struggle or whose lives they hurt. They were more interested in stopping the Viet Nam war and dethroning Nixon than they were in the Civil Rights Movement. Causing a racial war was just another tool to accomplish their goals, and if people died—all the better. I learned in the aftermath of it all that one of them had a gun and had planned to use it against the police that night.

We theorized that the Dean of the College—an ex-military man of twenty years—was alerted by an anonymous informant in our midst about our plans, and The Dean allegedly had the BSU meeting room bugged which enabled him to know exactly when to call in the cops.

With guns pointed at our heads, we were corralled into the BSU meeting room, made to sit against the wall while sitting on our hands during the interrogation, and then—suddenly—without explanation or warning, we were let go—no finger printing, no arrests. In a paranoid era when President Nixon was compiling a list of renegade colleges and universities for his **President's Commission on Campus Unrest,** the aborted BSU takeover at my college managed to go unnoticed and unreported. It is one of the best kept secrets of the time that a religious school that pretended to be A-O.K. with its Negro students was, without a doubt, bringing up the rear of the integration train in the north in the name of Jesus. But given the Kent and Jackson State alternatives—for whatever reason—my time as a student during those volatile years turned out to be very lucky, because I am convinced I would have lost my life that night had the takeover gone down as planned by the manipulative radicals within our midst.

✠

I am discovering that being thrown into a strange and competitive environment on a wing and a prayer takes everything you've got. Who knew there would be hidden monsters in the guise of friends and foes who were waiting to come out to play at my bastion of learning?

By the end of four long years, I did graduate with excellent grades and a degree in music, but I was broken in spirit, excruciatingly lonely, painfully aware I had nowhere to go once I graduated, and secretly afraid someone was going to expose the fact I didn't know Jack shit about much that I'd earned a degree in. During the summer of 1971, America's landscape was soaked with the blood of the good and the innocent: Martin, John, Bobby, Medgar, and Malcolm. I had been educated, but to what end? Where would I go, what would I do, and why the fuck did I even exist? After a while, something had to give in my psyche. All the personal monsters I'd encountered in childhood collided with my fear of the national monsters that were appearing right and left, and overwhelmed by anxiety, I had a nervous breakdown.

13

Change Mah Name

~

"I tol' Jesus He could change mah name.
And Jesus tol' me your father
won't know you
If I changed your name.
But I tol' Jesus it would be alright
If He changed mah name."
(Traditional Negro Spiritual/circa
1850s)

Do you know what I've discovered? I hate pudding!
My sister Pee-wee hates it too. We both hate pudding
because of our crazy-ass mother. It was her favorite
dessert to make and we could never tell from its surface how many lumps were hidden underneath. We
could never tell if the whole damn thing curdled in
the making or was destined to be curdled from its
inception.

⋇⊗⋇

On one very snowy day before Queen Maxine kicked us out of her boarding house, Mama seemed completely lucid and somewhat normal. She was so clearheaded and joyful she actually offered to make Pee-wee and me something magical out of snow. At seven years old I couldn't believe that snow could be turned into a tasty treat, but I was over the moon with excitement at the promise of it.

Mama mixed some type of powder from a box with milk and eggs and cooked it on the stove. When the mixture had cooled down, we breathlessly followed her upstairs and watched as she reached out the second story window of the bedroom we all shared and dug deep into the newly fallen snow on the porch roof below. She filled several large bowls with mounds of fresh snow. Giving me one of the bowls while she carried the others, the three of us marched in a ceremonial parade down the steps into the kitchen like the three magi bearing gifts to the King—Mama in the lead bearing two bowls of white gold, Pee-wee in the middle crawling backwards down the stairs like a malfunctioning wind-up toy, and me bringing up the rear with my final gift of frozen frankincense and myrrh.

Pee-wee and I could barely contain our exuberance as we sat at the kitchen table while Mama made a big show of folding the cooled yellow mixture from the stove into the bowls of snow. She told us this was a secret recipe her Cherokee mother had taught her how to make, and now she wanted to pass the secret on to us. When the frozen mounds had married with the yellow, gravy-like liquid, Mama gave Pee-wee and me two huge bowls of something called "Frozen Custard Cream." As Mama beamed with glowing satisfaction at the ambrosia she had whipped up for her children, Pee-wee and I dove into the anticipated nectar of the gods with great gusto. But as we began to eat the custard, we both stared at each other in horrific surprise and engaged in a synchronized vomit storm caused by our attempts to swallow the pasty, curdled lumps that were the size of engorged leeches hidden beneath the shiny surface of the custard.

The more we tried to swallow the custard and ignore the lumps, the sicker we became because the lumps were enormous and unavoidable. Pee-wee started projectile vomiting all over the table and that made my gag reflex even worse. When we both shoved the inedible custard away from us as if it were poison, Mama got really angry and attacked poor Pee-wee. While shooting me a controlling death-ray look that resulted in me swallowing the offensive sludge, she grabbed Pee-wee's mouth and tried to shove the custard down her throat. I managed to gulp it down, but Pee-wee just couldn't do it. The more our enraged mother tried to force the custard back into Pee-wee's mouth, the more it squirted out of every one of Pee-wee's orifices.

In later years when Pee-wee and I would talk about our innate hatred of all foods with lumpy DNA (pudding, grits, oatmeal, cream of wheat, rice and tapioca pudding), we figured out that Mama was fooled by the shiny, smooth, custardy surface that hid the curdled surprise underneath.

※❈※

When I crawled into the corner of my dorm room during the last month of my senior year—smashed between my bed and the wall—I cried for three days. I didn't eat, I didn't sleep, and I just sat in darkness while my curdled psyche exposed itself to me like the insides of Mama's pudding. Any armchair psychiatrist could have diagnosed the pain I felt in every fiber of my being. The abuse and abandonment of my childhood fused with the slights, rejections, betrayal, racism, and contempt I'd experienced at college. The marriage of these torments had produced lumps of overwhelming fear, soul-crushing loneliness, and debilitating feelings of incompetence. They launched an assault on my sanity—like maggots devouring the last vestiges of a carcass.

For the first time in my life I began to question why I existed, and if I had a place in the scheme of things. I had escaped the East Side of Cleveland. I had gotten an education and survived the Affirmative Action abyss ("We can boast that we offered them a seat at the table, but if they flunk out, we can say they were incapable of digesting the food set before them."). But

I had no idea what to do with my life. Where did I belong? Where should I go? What was my next step? Sometimes in life, the best we can do is take one step at a time out of the place that binds us and hope it leads to someplace better. I wiped my tears away, got up off the floor, stuffed the scary curds back into the recesses of my mind, and knocked on the next door that appeared before me.

※※

"Hello, I am one of the actors in a drama at the new amphitheater in your town. I understand you have an apartment to rent for the summer, and you are making it available to the cast and crew of the show. Would you mind if I drop by and take a look at the apartment?" I said, reading from the script in front of me.

"Why absolutely," answered the slight southern drawl of the white woman on the other end of the phone. "In fact, you don't have to worry about looking anywhere else, 'cause I can just tell by your sweet voice that you and me are gonna hit it off like two peas in a pod. Come on down, honey, just as soon as you can—you hear!"

Every phone conversation started out that way in my attempt to locate housing for the summer in an all-white southern Ohio town. This was one of the small towns hosting the beginning of a mega outdoor drama that had been established to bring hundreds of thousands of tourist dollars to the area. I had gotten a job as an actress with an international cast and crew right after I graduated from college. But all my site visits with the landladies and lords ended with a slammed door in my face and similar proclamations across the board.

"You don't look like you sounded on the phone, that's for sure. If I had known you were a nig . . . a Colored person, I wouldn't have told you that I'd rent to you."

One Good Samaritan capped off my penultimate search very succinctly by saying what the others didn't have the courage to say: "Listen, girlie; I'm gonna do you a favor. Nobody in this town is gonna rent to a nigger. Do yourself a favor, and go on back to where you came from, if you know what's good for you."

I had lucked into an acting job along with a black male student and several white students from my college. We would be working with a Canadian director and a cast and crew from other parts of the world, and none of them were prepared for the entrenched racial hatred in an area of Ohio that was rumored to have the largest KKK membership in the nation at that time. The entire cast had readily found places to rent—all except my male counterpart and me.

The little town that didn't have one black person living within its borders seemed to have three churches on every corner, and most of the churches were affiliated with the religious sect of my college. Having nothing to lose, I went back to my school and decided to shame The Choir Director whose son may or may not have still been in the closet.

"You owe me, old man," I said as all two-hundred pounds of me stormed into The Choir Director's office. "You not only owe me for the way you let your son humiliate me in front of the choir about something I believe you now know to be true, but one of your student helpers spilled the shit to me about how hypocritical you are. He told me that from here to Florida and from England to Holland, you sent notifications ahead of our concert performances to alert people that you were traveling with a certain amount of Negroes. I'm told that special arrangements were made beforehand to house us out of sight and behind the scenes. Seems this school is not the place of racial equality and harmony you love to boast about in your recruiting brochures when you're trying to get quality voices for your fucking showcase choir. So here's the deal: My Mentor's husband is a photographer at one of Cleveland's leading newspapers. You either work your low-life magic to get the "Negroes" a place to live in that religious KKK town, or I will expose the racial discord on this campus that you and this administration have tried so hard to keep under wraps."

"All the Negroes" who came to the southern Ohio town to act and sing for the summer had housing within a week—provided by the churches affiliated with my alma mater and instigated by a white teacher who thought he had invited Eleanor into his choir but ended up getting Pipsqueak in the bargain.

❋❋

As I peered through the screen door at the young, frail-looking white woman in front of me, she couldn't seem to decide whether to unlatch the door and let me in, or slam the door in my face and go hide under the bed. After a couple minutes of awkward silence, a high-pitched Tennessee accent tenuously said, "Hi, I'm Mary-Kate and I'm a Christian—I hope you don't mind."

I sullenly said: "Hi, I'm Eleanor; I'm here to see the apartment you have for rent."

I defiantly thought: "Oh shit, now I'm really fucked—a hillbilly, a bigot, and a religious fanatic."

❋❋

Mary-Kate turned out to be married to Billy-Bob, and they were school teachers with two small children who had just recently moved to the area. They were also known in the town as the "Smokey Mountain Jesus Freaks." They and another family responded to a minister's challenge to open up their homes to the "invading Negroes." The minister's motivation had nothing to do with Christian charity but everything to do with commerce—he knew the money generated by the new amphitheater would be a benefit to the entire town, and the color green will always trump the color of bigotry if you get enough greedy people in the mix.

I was very foreign to my new landlords, and I have reason to believe they were a little afraid of me. I sported a huge Afro in the style of the radical Angela Davis, and the years of hurt and anger accessorized everything I said and did. My landlords had no idea how to talk to me, or what to do with me, so they made a conscious decision to treat me with respect and kindness. From the very beginning, they invited me into their home and made me a part of their family as if I were a long-lost relative. Even though I lived upstairs in the third-floor apartment of their beautiful Victorian home, I found myself gravitating towards them in the mornings and evenings to share meals or a cup of coffee because I enjoyed their company so much. We began to open up our lives like the pages of two well-worn books, and as we did, we discovered we had more in common than not. They had grown up poor in America, fought hard to be educated, and felt just as disenfranchised from the American Dream as I did. I learned about the sufferings of poor whites in Tennessee which didn't seem too dissimilar from the sufferings of poor blacks in Cleveland.

Hippies and Jesus Freaks hitchhiking across the country would roll into town and always find a place to crash in my hosts' home. On any given evening when I returned from my performance shortly after midnight, there would be a handful of ragamuffins hanging out in their living room discussing the meaning of life and singing songs that spoke of their search for truth and their love of God. This young couples' love for me and the strangers they nourished began to have a profound effect on me. My landlords made the wretched and the poor a part of their family, as they had done with me, and never cared about what it cost their standing in the community. It took all summer, but the pain inside me began to dissolve a little bit like mounds of snow on the first day of spring, and I began to let go of the fear and anger that had so utterly consumed me.

❈❈❈

I've only had one deeply transcendent, truly life-transforming mystical experience in my entire journey, and it happened in the summer of 1971 in the home of the Smokey Mountain Jesus Freaks who were as surprised as I was when the scene went down.

I had only a week left before the outdoor drama would come to a close, and I knew I'd end up in the same place I had been two months before: no place to go, no job to go to, and no clue as to where I belonged. As I was passing through my hosts' living room one morning on the way to the breakfast nook as I had done all summer long, I noticed there was a glass jewelry box on the mantle of the fireplace. The box was so beautiful I slowed down to examine it.

There was a stunning ring in the glass box that consisted of a large purple amethyst stone encircled by smaller lavender blush stones. Next to the ring was a note folded into a small square in the manner of notes that used to be passed amongst kids in high school. Assuming it was private, I never opened the glass box nor did I read the note, but it did pique my interest as to its placement on the mantel. I had admired that ring when Mary-Kate had worn it on special occasions, and I was slightly puzzled by its new home. She had told me it was a family heirloom.

After my show was over that night, I returned to the house and went downstairs to unwind with my hosts, only to discover they had a living room full of people. Most of them had guitars and were sitting on the floor playing and singing various folk songs. I grabbed a cup of tea and sat on a window seat across the room from the group—enjoying the music and planning to depart once they started their usual conversations about God. I was lost in my own thoughts, trying to sort out what was going to happen with my life in a few days.

Suddenly, as I was staring out the window, I saw a flash of light in the reflection of the glass and looked over my shoulder into the room to see what it was. The light was an all-consuming bright essence in the center of the room that caused everything and everyone to seem to fade into the background. No one else seemed to see the light. The people on the floor kept chatting and singing as I stared at the radiance across the room. And then a voice called my name and it didn't sound like anything I'd ever heard before.

"Eleanor—will you surrender?" the crystal-clear voice said in my head and heart.

Like the goddess Athena, who planted ideas in Odysseus' head all through his odyssey and then appeared to him in the end disguised as a little girl who led him home, I knew this voice had been with me all my life. But I'd never heard it this distinctively. It seemed to be calling me—to a new name—to a new place.

The voice seemed to come from somewhere deep within and call to something far beyond my earthly existence. Soon I heard gut-wrenching sobs cascading into the room. The crying went on for thirty minutes or so, and it took some time before I realized the broken-hearted sobs were coming from me. When it was all over, no one moved for a long time. Finally, Mary-Kate got up and went to the fireplace mantel and brought back the glass box I had seen earlier. Trembling to the point of almost dropping the jewelry box, she handed it to me and asked that I read the note inside.

Eleanor—I know this may be hard to believe but, when I woke up this morning I had a strong feeling I should give you this family heirloom as a going away present. I also felt that today God would reveal himself to you in a way you could understand, and he would give you the chance to surrender the pain that has tormented you all your life in exchange for his love. Please accept this ring as a reminder of the day when your heart and eyes were opened and you saw a glimpse of God. As you continue on your life's journey and start to think that what you've heard and seen might have been an illusion—remember that on this day, something powerful and concrete really happened to you. You were born for a reason and you are deeply, deeply loved.—Love, Mary-Kate

※❈※

Waking up on a morphine drip after having a life-threatening operation couldn't have produced a more euphoric feeling than I felt the next morning. There was no pain—just an all-consuming love for everything from the tree outside my window to my worst enemy. In the days that followed, I sent a letter to The Choir Director at my college and thanked him for allowing me to see the world and asked his forgiveness for my having been so abrasive towards him. He was no less a bigot, but I had a suspicion that my healing lay in the path of taking responsibility for my own bitterness and spite. I let go of the suspicion that my mother's insanity might hold sway over me in the future. I wrote the Sperm-spewer and the Cheese Man's names on pieces of paper and physically shredded the memory of them, as I flushed the papers down the toilet. *I surrendered my fear of all the monsters from my past.* I had an epiphany that I was operating under a new name now—neither my mother nor my father's name—but my own name, and attached to it was a calling. I just needed to go about finding out what it was. I had a sixth sense that healing lay in the direction of searching for my spiritual evolution, and I knew I couldn't afford to miss that journey. I went by way of New York City for a year, did the starving artist trip, and walked away from it all into a community of people looking for similar healing. My destiny took a path less traveled that would dramatically change my life forever, and it all started in a town that hadn't even wanted me to live within its borders.

※※

I am discovering that there are two spiritual truths espoused by others older and wiser than I that are like lighthouse beams in the night for every hurting and discouraged heart.

"God comes to us disguised as our life."—**Richard Rohr**
"People see God every day; they just don't recognize Him."—**Pearl Bailey**

14
What's Love Got To Do With It?

~

"First best is falling in love. Second best is being in love. Least best is falling out of love. But any of it is better than never having been in love."— **Maya Angelou**

Do you know what I've discovered? Love works when we put another person's needs ahead of our own.

❈❈

"Black folks don't drop out to find themselves. We're barely in, child," said The Head Clerk who had transitioned into My Mentor/Mother and who I affectionately called "MM." I was on the phone with her trying to explain why I was leaving New York City and the pursuit of an opera career after she had worked so hard to help me leapfrog out of poverty and ignorance.

"Well, what about your voice teachers—the two in Ohio and the one in New York City? Have you told them you're leaving the promise of an opera career to go live on a farm with a bunch of spoiled white kids?"

"MM, I wouldn't call schlepping across the country as a minimum wage chorus gypsy with a mediocre touring company a promising career. Nor would I call the vague promise of a Julliard Studio scholarship a concrete lead. If you really want to know, I think the Julliard carrot was Madame Lila's bait to try and keep me in New York City to maintain her cash flow, because I'm just not that good. It takes a lot of students to pay the rent on a music studio above Carnegie Hall for a seventy-year-old teacher."

"Regardless, what did your voice teachers say?" insisted MM.

"My Cleveland voice teacher never responded, which really hurt me if the truth be known. I think she doesn't know what to say. This isn't something I can sing, it has to be lived. I haven't told my college voice teacher yet because Madame Lila was her teacher, and she pulled a lot of strings to get me on Lila's teaching schedule, not to mention convincing her old teacher to charge me half the going rate."

"As far as Madame Lila is concerned, she argued against my decision for forty-five minutes during my final voice lesson. She said, 'God lives in New York City too—I'm a Jew and I should know. I have God—who needs to go to a farm with a bunch of dirty hippies to

find God? *Are you meshuganah?*' When she saw her argu-
ments were to no avail and my lesson time was up, she
literally ripped her blouse in anguish and refused to
speak to me again. Then she symbolically pronounced
me dead to her, turned her back on me, and sat Shiva."

Looking back, it must have seemed to all concerned that I was being horrifically ungrateful, but
they weren't wrestling with the demons that I was. I
may have seen the light of salvation at Mary-Kate and
Billy-Bob's, but I still had the specter of my mother's
madness frantically buzzing inside my head like flies
stuck to a fly trap, and that scared the hell out of me. I
needed time to pull back, slow down, and nurture the
growth of my inner being.

✷✷

During the late 60s and early 70s, ashrams, communes,
and religious communities started sprouting up all
over the country, and they were alluring to the idealistic hippies who wanted to forge a deeper relationship
with the "spiritual world" and live lives that were less
materialistic. My friends Mary-Kate and Billy-Bob sold
everything they had and moved to a religious community that was located on a farm in the Northeast. When
they wrote and invited me to visit their new home, the
debilitating loneliness that was crippling me as I tried
to make it in New York dissipated as soon as I experienced the communal living that was part of their new

lifestyle. I had never milked a cow before, and I had never helped cook meals for scores of strangers just dropping in to "hang-out for a while." It was exhilarating to be part of a group of people that were so vulnerable and open and committed to a higher calling to help others. Here was a place I felt I could settle for a while and begin to heal.

As in most communes during that time, we were a wild and woolly bunch: a group of misfits made up of predominantly white kids from rich and middle class families. There were run-away sons and daughters of preachers, teachers, and corporate heads, a once famous girl-group alumna with five Top 40 hits, a narcissistic leader driven by a desire to be adulated and adored, Easy Riders and beauty queens, valedictorians and high school drop outs, peaceniks and worn-out Vietnam vets, semi-famous rock guitarists and not-so-famous actors and dancers. Most of us were young, spiritually starving or bankrupt, and looking for the fathers and families that had never stepped up to the plate. Add to that mix two and a quarter black people, one Chinese person, two grandmothers, and a great grandmother, and the picture is pretty much complete regarding the religious community whose port I sailed into.

A lot of good happened in our midst, and a lot of people were helped along the way—especially me, because the lessons I learned about prayer and meditation would become the cornerstone of my healing. We caught the vision (if only for a moment) of "all for one and one for all" as we shared everything we had for the common good and tried to treat each other as sisters and brothers. But in the end, we failed each other. In looking back on the eleven years I spent in The Community, I now see that we suffered the fate of most communal groups from that era—imploding because we became too myopic, and our human nature trumped our desire to love each other unconditionally. Somewhere along our idealistic journey, leaders over-stepped their boundaries, friends betrayed each other, duplicitous lives were exposed, and as all two year olds soon discover—sharing loses its luster as one gets older. We began to long for our own space, our own houses and "stuff," while human nature declared in more ways than one: "This is mine—it sucks for you if you don't have what I have—but tough titty!" It turns out that it was easier to preach a way of selfless living than it was to actually live it. In the end, disillusionment, bitterness, broken-heartedness, and resentment were the poison pills that destroyed our youthful vision. None of that ended up mattering much to me because even though I didn't know it when I arrived at The Community, one of the major reasons my journey had led me there was because a perfect suitor would come my way.

✳❈✳

"There's nothin' no white man can do for me," I said as I peeled potatoes alongside a couple of other women in The Community. "Sure, I'm working out life with a bunch of white people here, but it doesn't mean I would ever want to sleep with one of them—I can't even imagine!"

"Well you're in for a rude awakening," said my Chinese friend. "We average about one black guy every three years through here and at that rate you'll end up marrying these brown potatoes before you ever find a man."

"Yeah, well I've got a list of what I want in a man, and I pray for him to appear every day," I said. "He's got to be smart. He needs to be an actor/singer so that we have something in common; but most of all, he has to adore me and treat me like a queen. The man has got to be good father potential, and have a colossal sense of humor. After what I've been through in life—settling for less is not an option."

"Don't forget to add to your list that he has to be black," said another friend, who was black and laughed as she chopped up the bucket of potatoes to be mashed. "Because if you forgot to add that detail, I just want to let you know that God has a great sense of humor and you're probably screwed."

❊❊

Even though I had been a fat girl most of my life, I never had any problems getting a date, except during a dry spell in college. I had a date for both my junior and senior proms, and I even had a couple of serious boyfriends in high school. But when you're the fat girl who has come out of an abusive past, you become "that girl" from whom the guys are after only one thing, until you reach a point when you can't take it anymore. Then you kick their asses to the curb and crawl up in a corner and read—cultivating your love affair with Dickens, Angelou, and Hughes. Somehow, I always knew I deserved better than the suitors being served up by life, and I gambled that it would be better to be alone than in a mediocre relationship or marriage. I'd learned that much from Penelope, and I just kept waiting for my Odysseus to show up.

※※

To say that I fell in love with WW ("White and Wonderful") the first time I saw his face would be a lie. It was his voice. I fell in love with his voice when I overheard him auditioning for a play that our repertory theater company was getting ready to mount. His voice was so deep and mellifluous that I thought he was black, and I hurried down the hallway and up into the darkened balcony of the theater to sneak a peek at the new guy. By the time we actually came face to face, the healing that started on the inside had manifested on the outside—I had morphed into a size-six beauty that made WW truly stand up and take notice.

The new guy was blonde with nebbish-looking glasses, and he was wicked smart. I would later learn that he was a direct descendent of Governor Bradford of the Mayflower. He had graduated with honors from a top-notch high school, entered college at seventeen and finished in three years as a *magna cum laude* student, spoke Russian and French, and studied in the Soviet Union at the height of the Cold War.

On our second date we stayed up all night talking and found that we came from very different worlds. The only white people who had visited me in my home(s) were slum landlords and the various Miss Perkinses, but the only black person who had ever come to WW's childhood home was the "colored" mailman. But even then, WW only saw his back as he scurried away because the family dog was racist and always chased the poor letter carrier down the street before he could halfway deposit the mail. I still tease him about that family dog and the borderline racist comment WW made on our third date: "Your English is almost perfect—you're so articulate. The only thing I can tell that is missing is the subjunctive, which most people have a hard time with. Let me introduce you to that little stickler and you'll be good to go!"

WW was duly horrified by my life story. But his family seemed like a "Leave It to Beaver" episode— until I looked deeply into his eyes. What I saw there was a life that had been lived more in the "Twilight Zone."

"If you come from such a perfect family, why do your eyes look so sad?" I asked. "You are the saddest looking white man I've ever met. I know why most Black folks are sad—what's your excuse?" He cried as he told me about all of the pain that he kept hidden inside from the ravages of a childhood spent in a dysfunctional family, and I cried with him. Even though we came from different worlds, I totally understood his pain and the desire to be healed. One of the gifts we found in each other was the ability to see humor in the most unlikely places which has been a tool that has enabled us to overcome subsequent monsters we've encountered on our journey together.

※❀※

I married my suitor six years later. We didn't wait because we couldn't handle the interracial hurdle but because it would take that amount of time for WW to navigate the gnarliness of the pain caused by a tyrannical ball-buster of a mother (who hated me), a weak alcoholic father (who adored me, in spite of his wife's dictates), and all the childhood monsters that had come out to play in his life while he was growing up. I would need those six years to learn how to overcome my wariness of fully trusting another human being. The trust was a step-by-step process, and there was a time within those six years that I dumped poor WW because he "wasn't black enough," until I realized the issue wasn't race but believing that my future husband would be there for me and not abandon me as my father had.

❊❊

"WW's parents aren't here yet and it is way past the time for the mother of the groom to be seated," said Pee-wee. "My bet is that she's having a hissy-fit and isn't going to show. I think the reality of a 'black daughter-in-law' is finally sinking in—she's probably halfway back home right now. Remember, this is the woman who wouldn't let your engagement picture be published in her hometown newspaper. If she couldn't handle a picture of your black face, how is she going to live through this wedding?" Pee-wee was my Maid of Honor and had grown into a stunningly beautiful woman—albeit a cynical one. Gone were the scars of Mama's abuse. My baby sister had a full head of gorgeous hair and flawless skin, and she was a picture of confidence. She had graduated from college and was working for a Fortune 500 company. We had become the yin and the yang of our common experiences: I always saw the glass half-full, and Pee-wee tended to see the glass half-empty.

"Oh, she'll show," said My Mentor, as she calmly adjusted the train on my wedding gown. "I know women like your soon-to-be mother-in-law. They're all about what other people think of them. The house could be falling down around them, but as long as the neighbors don't know what's going on, everything is perfect. There are hundreds of people here, and she'd have a lot of explaining to do to all of WW's relatives if she didn't show—not to mention that she'd have to deal with me if she ruined your wedding day."

My surrogate mother had become one of the great loves of my life. And even though she was initially puzzled by my move to The Community, she wrote me a letter two weeks after my arrival to let me know that she supported my choice. She understood where I'd come from, and she believed in me, and, "Oh, by the way, I'll be driving up with Pee-wee ASAP to make sure the place you've 'dropped into,' is not a cult."

My mother-in-law finally did show up, albeit her eyes were puffy from crying all night, and she looked like she was attending a funeral rather than a wedding. But I really didn't care what WW's mother thought. As the strains of Vivaldi's Concerto in D Major began to fill the room and ballet dancers performed an original choreographed dance under the wedding canopy, I couldn't stop smiling. Wearing the most magnificent wedding gown I'd ever seen, I marched down the aisle under an arch of palm branches (an ancient symbol of victory and triumph) formed by the dancers. When I reached the stage, I looked into the eyes of the most kind, handsome, and generous man I'd ever met, and I saw myself through those loving eyes. At that moment, I realized the monsters had been lying all along because WW's eyes radiated the truth that still shines through them to this day: *You are so beautiful, my African queen!*

Our religious community was at its finest that day. Everyone joyfully pulled together to become the family I never had. Because we were mostly artisans and artists, everything I needed *or wished for* was provided by them—everything from the catering to the photography, the original music to the honeymoon suite, and even the wedding cake. In spite of the massive disappointment we would later become to one another, on the most important day of my life a multitude of "brothers and sisters, cousins and aunts" genuinely cheered for the success of my journey with the man of my dreams. I will always love them for that.

※

I married WW on my 31st birthday. He promised to adore me, cherish me, and restore all that the cankerworm had eaten. I promised to honor him, respect him, and guard his heart against the slings and arrows of any monsters to come. WW's mother sobbed so loudly that she almost drowned out our vows. We tuned her out, and stared into each other eyes as his eyes said: *Ignore her—I choose you, I adore you, I love you!* My eyes said: *You are the one—today, tomorrow, and always.* I had never been so happy or felt so beautiful in my entire life, and being born in a toilet in Cleveland seemed like something far, far away and part of some-body else's story. It was a perfect day, and I had given myself the perfect birthday present. After a kiss that seemed to last forever and made the audience gasp, WW engulfed me with a glorious smile and said loud enough for the heavens to hear: *"Happy birthday, Honey!"*

※❀※

I am discovering that love can be found in the most unlikely places and with the most unexpected people. I am also discovering that you never know when the right suitor will show up and become a keeper. And I know these things to be true as well: unless the lovers are willing to give their all—holding nothing back—there will be no healing, no destinies joined, no hearts entwined, and no monsters thrown down.

Epilogue

~

"The one thing that you have that nobody else has is you. Your voice, your mind, your story, your vision. So write and draw and build and play and dance and live as only you can."—**Neil Gaiman**

※※

So this is my odyssey. In the eyes of many, I started out my journey as a *nobody—a ragamuffin*—and like everybody, I encountered my fair share of monsters in life. But now that I can see the long view, I can truly boast that *I am somebody* because I have a story of survival to tell.

Pee-wee and I went on to fulfill our dreams of living, educated, prosperous lives—she was prophetic that night in the police car: everything turned out to be more than all right. I have traveled throughout the world to places that I first only read about after discovering the library. My sister and I have never stopped holding each other's hand as we got older and grayer, and our grace and compassion towards each other has grown deeper through the years. We both married and tried to become the family we were never afforded by our parents as Pee-wee became the *Aunt Extraordinare* to my two daughters. My marriage to the "white man" who I thought couldn't do anything for me became the joy of my life, and after almost four decades, he still makes me laugh everyday, and my heart flutters when the garage door goes up indicating that he is returning home to me at the end of another day's journey.

All the monsters in my story have died (at least I hope they have). Most of the heroes have died as well, except for my mentor who is now in her eighties. We talk to each other every week and I never fail to thank her for looking beyond her own worries and limitations during the pre-Civil Rights days and reaching out to save me from the monsters at hand.

I am somebody because my life has proven that love, grace, restoration, hope, and joy, when supplemented by *boon companions,* can be found if we don't let the monsters kill us—if we don't let them define us. But maybe that is the reason for the existence of monsters after all—to make us stronger.

Acknowledgements

~

I am forever grateful to the following people for their support and encouragement during the writing of this memoir:

To Professor Ginny Garnett who didn't laugh at my pathetic first draft but told me I had a strong voice and encouraged me to keep writing.

To Kirsten Fatzinger and Deb Tomlin who were my first beta readers, and who suffered through the initial story and helped me realize that I had two books in one—saving my readers from all-out boredom and providing me with a sequel. They were some of my first cheerleaders. They guided the branding of the book, and their friendship has been invaluable throughout this process.

To Dr. Chris and Linda Christensen who were initial readers of the first daft; they checked the veracity of the retelling of our community days, and they read my virgin manuscript and didn't go screaming into the night.

To KLT, CDT (who happen to be my daughters), **CR** (the infamous Pee-wee), **Sondra Smith, Maxine Wilkins**, and **Alaise Rudder** who so graciously became part of my beta readers for the revamped book and whose suggestions made "my baby" stand up and be noticed.

To Joanne Smyth who lovingly agreed to become my editor and whose invaluable comments and fine-tuning of the text helped produce a memoir that I could really be proud of. There were times when I thought I'd lose my mind during this project, but she constantly pushed me onward and upward. (JS: I love you, dearly!)

And finally, to my husband "WW"—my frontline editor whom I sleep with, and the first one to tell me that I could write, who copyedited my manuscript countless times, and who was always there in the dark urging me on when I thought I couldn't reach my goal. ("WW" you are the love of my life, my champion, and my most trusted companion).

About the Author

~

Eleanor Tomczyk recently retired from the Brand Marketing department of a Fortune 500 company after having previously been a teacher, an actress, and a singer. An award-winning voiceover artist, she was under exclusive contract with one of the nation's leading television and radio production companies for voiceovers in national and regional commercials for eleven years. Eleanor is a humorist blogger with followers throughout the world at www.howthehelldidIenduphere.wordpress.com. The author has been married for almost four decades to "WW" (White and Wonderful) who is a major character in her blogs, and together they have two adult children, a grandson, and a grand dog. When Eleanor is not writing, she is traveling the world with WW and slaying the monsters that are stupid enough to try and get in her way.

Made in the USA
Lexington, KY
21 December 2013